BFI Modern Classics

Rob White
Series Editor

BFI Modern Classics is a series of critical studies of films produced over the last three decades. An array of writers explore their chosen films, offering a range of perspectives on the dominant art and entertainment medium in contemporary culture. The series gathers together snapshots of our passion for and understanding of recent movies.

Trainspotting

Murray Smith

 Publishing

For Thing One and Thing Two

First published in 2002 by the
British Film Institute
21 Stephen Street, London W1T 1LN

The British Film Institute promotes greater
understanding and appreciation of,
and access to, film and moving image
culture in the UK.

British Library Cataloguing-in-Publication Data
A catalogue record for this book is available
from the British Library

ISBN 0-85170-870-6

Series design by Andrew Barron &
Collis Clements Associates

Typeset in Italian Garamond and Swiss 721BT
by D R Bungay Associates, Burghfield, Berks

Printed in Great Britain by
The Cromwell Press, Trowbridge, Wiltshire

Contents

Acknowledgments

Writing this book has turned me into a *Trainspotting* trainspotter, and I am grateful to all those who have put up with my obsessive quest for arcane knowledge and the tiresome requests for information with which I have burdened friends, colleagues and total strangers. And never has a list been a more appropriate way of thanking the various individuals who have helped out, including David Boothroyd, Sarah Cardwell, Doug Farland, Simon Frith, Matthew Frost, Katie Grant, Michael Grant, Frances Guerin, Kevin Heffernan, David Herd, Charlie Keil, Guy Reynolds, Simon Reynolds, Robin Robertson, Jeff Smith, Goran Stefanovski, William Stow, Sarah Thornton, and not least, the Canterbury Hegelians. Thanks to my editor Rob White for the stick, the carrot, and various other methods of provoking me to write; and to the team at the BFI.

Miri Song, as ever, makes it all worthwhile. This book came together between the births of our sons Charlie and Theo, and I dedicate it to them.

1 Arriving

train-spotter
a. One (esp. a small boy) whose hobby is observing trains and recording railway locomotive numbers. Hence **train-spotting** *vbl. n*; **trains-spot** *v. intr.*
b. Also *transf.* (freq. *derog*), a person who enthusiastically studies the minutiae of any subject; a collector of trivial information.
main-line
1. a. The principal line of a railway.
b. A principal route, connection, conduit, family, etc
c. A large or principal vein, into which drugs can readily be injected; hence, an intravenous injection of drugs; the act or habit of making such an injection.
Oxford English Dictionary

Once upon a time, 'trainspotting' – spending endless hours watching for trains and ticking them off compendious lists – was a lowly, rather pathetic activity widely held in great contempt. Now, 'trainspotting' is a byword for cool. What happened?

The answer, in brief, is that Irvine Welsh wrote a novel called *Trainspotting*, on the basis of which screenwriter John Hodge, producer Andrew Macdonald and director Danny Boyle made a film called *Trainspotting*.[1] The film tells the story of five Edinburgh male twenty-somethings – Renton (Ewan McGregor), Spud (Ewen Bremner), Begbie (Robert Carlyle), Sick Boy (Jonny Lee Miller) and Tommy (Kevin McKidd) – and their larger circle of friends, relatives and associates. Almost all of them are 'schemies', their lives defined by the housing schemes in Leith, the poor port district of Edinburgh. The opening of the film plunges us directly into the hell-raising, transgressive lives led by the gang, as Renton, Spud and Sick Boy career through central Edinburgh, racing away from pursuing security guards. Renton's caustic voice-over puts the chase in context: 'Choose your future. Choose life. But why would I want to do a thing like that? I chose not to choose life, I chose somethin' else – and the reasons? There are no reasons. Who needs reasons when you've got heroin?'

These boys are junkies, and they run out of desperation and exhilaration. After a half-hearted attempt to come off the 'skag', the law catches up with Renton and Spud, an event which propels Renton more forcefully out of his

junkie orbit – as far as London. Tommy's death brings Renton back to
Edinburgh, where Begbie and Sick Boy cook up a plan for the gang to 'punt'
a large amount of heroin to a big-time dealer in London. Renton's second
visit to London proves altogether more decisive, the film ending as he walks
off into the sunrise – along with the stolen proceeds of the deal.

The novel *Trainspotting* was published in 1993. Initially published as a
small print run of 3,000, the novel far outstripped the expectations of both
its author and publisher, amassing sales of 100,000 copies by the time of
the film's release (doubtless helped along by a successful stage adaptation
of the novel). The high profile of the film helped to push the sales of the
novel to still another level; at the time of writing, total UK sales have
reached 800,000. The initial success of the novel can perhaps be
accounted for by its appeal both to a sector of the traditional literary
audience, appreciative of its exploration of dialect, its episodic form and
shifts of voice, as well as a 'non-literary' readership – an audience of club-
goers and music fans who recognised in the novel their generation, their
attitudes, their enthusiasms, their culture.

Trainspotting the film was released in February 1996 to considerable
hoopla, Welsh in effect giving his blessing to the project by taking on the
cameo role of dodgy dealer Mikey Forrester – who better to torture
Renton than the author of the original novel ('slow release – perfect for
your needs')? In terms of the nature of its production, *Trainspotting* was
significant for several reasons. The film emerged at a moment when not
only British cinema, but Scottish cinema, as a distinct entity, possessed an
unusual degree of visibility, activity and momentum. The previous year,
1995, witnessed the box-office success of two Scottish films, the historical

Irvine Welsh as Mikey
Forrester

epic *Rob Roy*, directed by Michael Caton-Jones, and the contemporary thriller *Shallow Grave*, the first feature by Macdonald, Hodge and Boyle, and the UK's highest-grossing British release of the year. *Shallow Grave* in turn became the springboard for the high-profile making of *Trainspotting* (financed – uniquely at the time – wholly by Channel Four, the budget of £1.7 million exceeding the company's investment in any other single film). The film was one of four new features in production over the course of 1995 which could lay claim to being Scottish. *Trainspotting* thus took its place at the centre of a resurgent Scottish cultural and political nationalism, consolidated by the establishment of the Scottish Parliament in 1998. It is worth remembering that when *Trainspotting* was released, the Tory government were about to enter the last, bitter year of what would ultimately be an eighteen-year reign of power in Britain. By this point Tory support in Scotland had entirely collapsed. The themes and values of *Trainspotting* are deeply marked by this era.

As a film emerging from a self-consciously nationalist context, based on a cult novel, and supported financially by Channel Four, one might have expected *Trainspotting* to be a typical piece of art cinema: sober, slowly paced, ostentatiously high-brow, 'challenging', directed to a relatively small audience. *Trainspotting* overturns most of these expectations, beginning with the level of its commercial success. *Trainspotting* took over £12 million at the UK box office, and went on to become the most successful independent release in the US in 1996, taking $16.5 million in box-office receipts by March 1997. These successes were echoed in many other countries; total worldwide returns thus far are estimated at $72 million. And yet it would not be wrong to see *Trainspotting* as an art film – albeit a kind of art film which tempers its high-cultural ambitions with a desire to reach a much broader audience than that traditionally associated with European art cinema. The model here is less European art cinema than the American art cinema tradition – not only the work of New Hollywood film-makers like Scorsese and Tarantino, but also that of earlier directors like Orson Welles, the bravura stylist whose legacy can be detected in *Trainspotting*.

The most obvious index of this desire for a large audience was the aggressive and canny marketing of the film. The film-makers exploited the worldwide interest in British popular culture in the mid-1990s, not only by basing the film on a novel arising out of that culture, but by constructing a soundtrack which mixed contemporary Britpop and dance tracks with some of the countercultural classics of the 1970s, thus tapping into the musical and fashion enthusiasms of several generations of potential viewers. The film's distributor, PolyGram Filmed Entertainment, launched an expensive publicity campaign (£850,000, or half as much as the film's production costs, for the UK launch) which resembled the heavy publicity associated with the Hollywood 'event' movie more than the modest campaigns associated with 'small' European releases. It is not hard to think of a 'high concept' pitch for the film: drug addiction with songs; *Drugstore Cowboy* (Gus Von Sant, 1989) meets *American Graffiti* (George Lucas, 1973); heroin as consumer choice. Indeed, the publicity for the film showed a wry awareness of its own nature, exhorting us to 'Believe the Hype!' Rather than using the channels and spaces typically used by the large American distributors, however, PolyGram invested in outlets and employed a design consultancy (Stylorouge) associated with pop and rock music culture. The company also collaborated with its competitor EMI in order to ensure an effective launch of the soundtrack CD tie-in.

Another sign of the film-makers' desire for a broad audience was the manner of the adaptation. Hodge has noted that the first difficulty he encountered in contemplating a screenplay was the episodic nature of the novel, splintered as it is through several characters, each narrating in their own idiolect. Hodge's solution – making Renton *the* central character, streamlining the story around him and fusing several other characters – is both ingenious, and a measure of the mainstream audience the film-makers were seeking. The shifts in character perspective and the somewhat fragmented structure of the novel are hardly unknown in film – indeed, they are staples of art cinema and 'indie' cinema, fully exemplified by Welsh's self-scripted *The Acid House* (Paul McGuigan, 1998). Nothing stopped Hodge, Macdonald and Boyle from pursuing a version of *Trainspotting* which retained the multiple perspective and vignette structure of Welsh's novel, other than their intuitive sense that such a film would be unlikely to reach a large audience,[2] and might compound the risk of the film becoming trapped in the 'drug film ghetto' occupied by self-consciously 'hardcore' drug films like *Christiane F.* (Uli Edel, 1981) and *Pusher* (Nicolas Winding Refn, 1996).

There can be no doubting the enormous cultural significance of *Trainspotting*, the impact of which still reverberates in Britain and beyond. The film acted as a lightning rod for debate across a wide array of social, cultural and aesthetic matters, including 'laddishness', male sexual inadequacy and musical and footballing obsessiveness. The idea of the 'New Lad' came to prominence in the early 1990s, marking a reassertion of traditional male values and prerogatives, following their abeyance in the 1980s (the decade of the sensitive 'New Man') and indeed in the wake of modern feminism as a whole. Some measure of the importance of this cultural trend can be gleaned from the rise of Nick Hornby, whose novels play variations on laddish, adolescent men coming up against and coming to terms with adult responsibilities and values. (More even than Welsh, Hornby made the trainspotterish list – 'Top five American films …' – the symbol of obsessive, self-involved masculinity.[3]) The successful television sitcom *Men Behaving Badly* (1992–7) dwelt in broader comic mode on the same tensions; and more broadly still, parodic comic *Viz* offered up Sid the Sexist and the Fat Slags, twinned figures of archaic, if knowing, misogyny. Laddism also took centre stage with the rise of Oasis, whose reputation often played up the beery pleasures of traditional masculinity, the Gallagher brothers seeming to relish rehashing every sorry cliché about the bad boys of rock 'n' roll.

But the tone of 'lad' culture has not been limited to the humorous. The vicious, predatory and sometimes narcissistic sexuality associated with this rejuvenated 'masculinism' was explored in many fictions, ranging from Mike Leigh's abrasive film *Naked* (1994) to *Trainspotting*'s Begbie and the

Diane, ladette

sinister television drama *Men Only* (2001). Other works focused on the sources of laddism in the dimunition of actual male power. Numerous films dealt with the phenomenon of working-class men displaced from their economic, and thus their social and psychological, roles, including *Raining Stones* (Ken Loach, 1993), *Brassed Off* (Mark Herman, 1996), *The Fully Monty* (Peter Cattaneo, 1997) and *Billy Elliot* (Stephan Daldry, 2000). These concerns intersected with anxieties about poverty, youth and class, especially in relation to the 'lawless' culture of council estates, isolated from an increasingly affluent middle class and trapped – economically and topographically – in areas of extraordinarily high levels of male unemployment. Following the riots and confrontations on housing estates in 1991 and 1992, joy-riding and ram-raiding became emblems of this emerging underclass of disaffected youth, the film *Shopping* (Paul Anderson, 1994) creating a vision of apocalyptic anomie.

The wider context for these anxieties was the idea that youth culture had entered a moment of exceptional disillusionment and diminished expectation, and turned its back as much on conventional forms of political protest as on mainstream existence. This notion was reflected in a range of new buzz words: the slacker, the loser, Generation X, and most pertinently here, 'the chemical generation' – a new youth counterculture revolving around clubbing, raves, and Ecstasy. The Criminal Justice Act of 1994 was a response not only to the civil unrest of the early 1990s in general, but specifically criminalised underground raves. This new counterculture was nowhere given more articulate expression than in the novels by Irvine Welsh which followed *Trainspotting*. The film of *Trainspotting* 'updated' the novel by incorporating a scene in which Renton and Begbie go to a rave, as well as several songs by dance and dance-rock acts, including Scots band Primal Scream, another important participant in the Scottish cultural renaissance. Welsh had collaborated with the band, providing lyrics for the single 'The Big Man and the Scream Team Meet the Barmy Army Uptown', while the band composed the instrumental 'Trainspotting', which appears in the film's patchwork of songs, underscoring Renton and Sick Boy's slack in the park. The combination of the film's intense colour scheme, pulsating soundtrack and kinetic style has been likened to the sensuous experience of contemporary clubbing.

Significant variations on laddism included the 'ladette' and 'geezer chic'. *Trainspotting* sports its very own ladette in the form of Diane (Kelly Macdonald), the main female character who downs shots in a single gulp, picks up and rejects men unapologetically, boots Renton out of her bed once she's had her sexual way with him, and leers out at us in the film's publicity material alongside four of the film's men. Diane lives it up with the same sense of entitlement and bravado as any lad. Her presence finds an echo on the soundtrack, in the androgynous shape of Elastica's Justine Frischmann, another woman clearly in control, orchestrating the sinewy cross-rhythms of '2:1'. The notion of 'geezer chic', meanwhile, crystallised around Guy Ritchie's *Lock, Stock and Two Smoking Barrels* (1998) and *Snatch* (2000). Taking their cue from the work of Quentin Tarantino and adapting it to the British cultural landscape, these films celebrated traditional masculinity in a highly stylised fashion, with a gallery of (mostly) East End types, from wide boys to weary bosses to gnarled old bouncers, peopling a narrative of baroque intricacy. A new cycle of gangster films gathered pace, including *Gangster No. 1* (Paul McGuigan, 2000) and *Sexy Beast* (Jonathan Glazer, 2000). Even Steven Soderbergh's *The Limey* (1999) was informed by the glamour of the Cockney bloke, appropriating footage of a young Terence Stamp in Ken Loach's *Poor Cow* (1967) as flashback material (and juxtaposing Stamp with a figure of parallel iconic status from 1960s American cinema, Peter Fonda). The London of the 'Swinging Sixties' hovers insistently behind this trend. *Trainspotting*, once again, was in on the act early, with its contrast between the nervous, callow 'skag boys' from Edinburgh, and the wry, menacing professional dealer played by Keith Allen (in a near-reprise of his role in *Shallow Grave*), along with the film's many stylistic allusions to 1960s London.

Trainspotting invokes the 1960s through its music and visual design. One of the most important 'voices' in the film's soundtrack is that of Britpop, the self-consciously British brand of rock music which achieved international prominence in the 1990s, through bands like Blur, Oasis and Pulp. Like so many contemporary movements, however, Britpop bands were acutely aware of the past – in this case, their inheritance from earlier waves of British pop and rock music, above all the bands associated with the British pop boom of the 1960s (the Beatles, the Rolling Stones, the Kinks, the Small Faces), and the (mostly British) punk and new wave acts of the late 1970s (the Buzzcocks, Wire, XTC, Blondie). Completing the circuit of allusion between the worlds of film and music, Blur's definitive Britpop song, 'Parklife' (1994), features a voice-over by Phil Daniels, fifteen years earlier the star of 1960s-set mod-film *Quadrophenia* (Franc Roddam, 1979). Daniels 'stars' in the song as a Cockney layabout killing time in a park, in a scenario redolent of the scene in *Trainspotting* in which Renton and Sick Boy loaf around with an air rifle (see p. 49).

Visually, nods to the 1960s are evident in touches reminiscent of Richard Lester's zany, anti-realist Beatles' films, *A Hard Day's Night* (1964) and *Help!* (1965), along with a shot which restages the cover pose of the Beatles' *Abbey Road* album, in which the members of the respective groups stride single-file over a London street. At times, with the continuous flow of pop music on the soundtrack and the various

Alluding to *Abbey Road*

permutations of the gang in locomotion, the film seems like a pop film in which the gang have taken on the role of pop group (leading to the exaggerated charge that the film presents 'heroin addiction as rock 'n' roll mythology: live fast, die young …').[4] The legacy of the punk movement, meanwhile, is evident not only in much of the film's music, but in the ragged, improvisational dress-style of Renton, Spud and Sick Boy, and above all in the iconoclastic, (spit-)in-your-face attitude of the gang.

These influences come together in the film's spiritual kinship with its exact contemporary in the art world, Young British Art. Like *Trainspotting*, Britart recalls the 1960s, in its case through the revival of Pop and conceptual art. And just as *Trainspotting* exemplifies a punchy, slick and commercially savvy rethinking of 1960s European art cinema, so Britart is distinguished by its unabashed desire to occupy the centre, rather than merely the margins, of culture. *Trainspotting* shares with Britart the combination of a flashy, self-promotional style; a dark and sometimes grotesque humour, which is nevertheless alive to the unexpected places and ways in which beauty can be found; and an effort to join cult cachet and mainstream success, intelligence and accessibility, complexity and directness. The most concrete connection between the film and Britart is the soundtrack presence of Blur and Pulp, contemporary exemplars of art school rock. Indeed, at least one biographical thread can be traced between *Trainspotting* and the YBAs: not long after Damien Hirst made the video for Blur's 'Country House', Blur agreed to contribute to the soundtrack of the film.[5]

Just as there were both comic and serious treatments of masculinity in British culture of the 1990s, so its depictions of heroin use were double-edged. On the one hand, some representations fed into what became known as 'heroin chic', a term coined in the US to describe the trend in

Damien Hirst, *With Dead Head* (1991, black and white photograph on aluminium, 22½ x 30 inches, courtesy Jay Jopling/White Cube, London)

the worlds of advertising and fashion for emaciated models exhibiting unfocused, glazed looks, 'their habit presented as succulently degenerate, edgy and alluring'.[6] Many films deployed drug use as a plot device with little interest in exploring drug experience, but few fiction films can be charged with a naïve, one-dimensional aestheticisation of addiction. Certainly this is not true of *Trainspotting*, even if Renton does possess a 'junkie-waif' demeanour.[7] While the film offers up its main characters as appealingly candid in their rejection of mainstream pieties and their embrace of heroin as an immediate alternative, it hardly shrinks from depicting the ghastly probable costs of addiction. *Trainspotting* rather lies in the tradition of pop songs like Morrissey's 'Interesting Drug' and Pulp's 'Sorted for E's and Wizz', which take a candid but ambivalent stance towards their subject matter, acknowledging 'the sheer omnipresence and banality of recreational drug use'.[8] While *Trainspotting* eschews moralistic condemnation of heroin – this is the thrust of Boyle's claim that the film takes 'no moral attitude' – it is hardly morally indifferent.[9]

One of the potential costs of heroin addiction was contraction of the HIV virus through shared, contaminated needles. As a city in which intravenous heroin use had mushroomed in the early 1980s, it was almost inevitable that Edinburgh would be blighted by the AIDS epidemic. This is the context of Tommy's story in the film, a story given grim irony by the fact that at the outset Tommy is clean and disinclined to use heroin; his relatively brief career as an addict results in his early death from an AIDS-related illness, while the film's persistent, hardcore users – Renton, Sick Boy and Spud – manage to evade infection.

By tradition Edinburgh is thought of as the civilised city of the Edinburgh Festival, counterposed in the popular imagination with the industrial legacy and sectarian hooliganism of Glasgow (I suspect that many non-Scottish viewers of the film, ignorant of local geography, mistake the Edinburgh of the film for Glasgow). Debunking this myth became common cause for many Scottish artists. The novelist James Kelman – whose use of phonetically rendered regional and class-specific voice was an important influence on Welsh – was denounced by civic leaders for besmirching Scotland's image. Welsh's contemporary, the crime novelist Ian Rankin, has spoken of his interest in revealing the 'hidden Edinburgh' beneath the 'genteel surface', and Welsh himself has noted that 'Tourists want to come to the Athens of the North rather than the HIV capital of Europe … and thus the people who suffer from HIV [are] deemed implicitly detrimental to tourism … So the schemes are taken out of existence.'[10] At its height, things were so bad in Edinburgh that Oxfam ran supplies into certain estates. To put it in the terms that I will come to use in this book, Rankin and Welsh were both interested in exposing the 'garbage' that lies within, or beyond the pale of, 'heritage' Edinburgh. Ironically, however, these critical voices and alternative visions were fast being swept under the umbrella of 'Cool Britannia', a government-led effort to hitch contemporary, often socially critical, British culture to the heritage bandwagon.

'I'm searchin' for my mainline', sang Lou Reed in 1968.[11] A whole cluster of train-related metaphors have long existed within drug culture (tracks and tramlines for puncture marks; mainlining and tracking for intravenous injection; riding the train for cocaine use). This imagery has existed parallel with, but separate from, the classic image of the trainspotter[12] – until the advent of *Trainspotting*, which conjoined them. So on the one hand, we have the rather sad, but innocent, pre-pubescent business of watching for trains and checking them off a vast list; and on the other, shooting up. *Trainspotting* fuses these apparently distant activities around the notion of male obsessiveness and the bored, dead-end existence that it accompanies, casting an air of innocence on the heroin addict, a shroud of pessimism on the spotty list-checker. But what about the *actual* trains that criss-cross the film, beginning with the rattling tracks and horn heard over the film's title credit? What are *they* doing there? (Notably, the title is never explained in the film, a fact which accentuates its ambiguity and symbolic richness.) Do they merely echo the meanings so far discussed, or do they thicken the symbolic resonance of the title still further?

To be a trainspotter – in the literal sense – is to stand for hours, in the same place, watching trains go by. To board a train is to go somewhere, to move on. To move on is to open oneself up to change. Renton is the character who travels most often by train, and the film *Trainspotting* is above all his story, a story of reckless joy, desolation and self-reinvention.

2 Young Americans

A gang of skinny heroin addicts rush towards the camera as it tracks back rapidly on a central street in Edinburgh, stolen goods dropping from them as they flee. After a second or so, the rhythm of their running is picked up and amplified by the pounding, dirty, raw opening of Iggy Pop's 'Lust for Life'. A moment later another layer of sound is added – the voice of Mark Renton as he intones a kind of heroin addict's manifesto, the first of the film's many lists, filled with confident contempt for all the material, conventional comforts he and his pals have forsaken for their true love, H: 'Choose life. Choose a job. Choose a career. Choose a family. Choose a fuckin' big television. Choose washing machines, cars, compact disc players and electrical tin openers … Choose rottin' away at the end of it all …'

These two sounds – McGregor's Scots diatribe on the one hand, the unmistakably American drawl of Iggy's voice on the other – provide a path into the complex inter- and intra-national dynamics of contemporary movie culture in general, and *Trainspotting* in particular. Iggy's presence and biography is a singularly appropriate one which pervades the narrative in more than the obvious ways (he crops up in the narrative and another of his songs, 'Nightclubbing', appears on the soundtrack). For Iggy is a junkie but also a survivor, the song 'Lust for Life' deriving from a period in the late 1970s when he emerged from a long drug-induced silence to produce two energetic albums. His wasted yet enormously durable frame, subjected to all manner of abuse and exertion – glimpsed in the background in a poster on Tommy's wall – matches perfectly the taut, pale skin of the Edinburgh smackheads. (McGregor went on to play the role of Curt Wild, a character clearly based on Iggy, in Todd Haynes's *Velvet Goldmine* [1998].) Iggy and 'Lust for Life' encapsulate the characters' and the movie's ambivalent attitude towards heroin – deliverer of both life-wrecking evil *and* delirious pleasure.

And yet Iggy is, of course, American, like so many of the reference points and (trainspotterishly indulged) enthusiasms of the film's central characters. Iggy is joined by fellow junkie-survivor Lou Reed, whose 'Perfect Day' provides semi-ironic accompaniment as Renton, deep in a heroin stupor, is taken to hospital by taxi and dumped outside it. The consumer items enumerated in Renton's litany were, of course, originally driven by the same society that produced Iggy and Lou. Elsewhere in the movie, a naïve American tourist in town for Edinburgh's most internationally well-known event – the Edinburgh Festival – is mugged by our friendly local skagheads. For all its 'Scottishness', the impact and appeal of America – its glamour and vitality – is everywhere in *Trainspotting*. Most elusively, the 'romanticism' of Renton's final break with the gang, his decision to ditch the past and reinvent himself in a new place, has a deep resonance with the American dream. This is, of course, a dream as much for non-Americans as Americans; as Lesley Fiedler once put it, the world is full of 'imaginary Americans'.

If the rest of the pop-music score is drawn from contemporary British bands, we shouldn't forget that, no matter how brilliantly and distinctively transformed by British traditions and stylings, such transformations – even

Iggy Pop/*Raw Power*
cover, London 1972
(copyright © Mick Rock,
1972, 2001)

those of Britpop – always carry with them the underlying 'Americanness' of rock as a musical form. Thus, the Estuary accents ('know wot I mean?') and greyhound racing cover photo of Blur's *Parklife* cohabit with a song called 'Magic America', which satirises the idea of America as a land of super-abundance, and an inside still from *The Graduate* (Mike Nichols, 1967). Similarly, while the sound of XTC stands behind the falsetto harmonies on 'Tracy Jacks' (another song on *Parklife*), doo-wop and Frankie Valli stand behind XTC.

The pervasive influence of American culture is also visually evident in *Trainspotting*. The film owes a debt to the visual flamboyance of the New Hollywood; Boyle has cited *A Clockwork Orange* (Stanley Kubrick, 1971) as an influence, and screened *The Exorcist* (William Friedkin, 1973), *Near Dark* (Kathryn Bigelow, 1987) and *Goodfellas* (Martin Scorsese, 1990) during pre-production; the subtitles which introduce each member of the male fraternity in the opening sequence specifically recall *Mean Streets* (Scorsese, 1973). *Trainspotting* also exemplifies the incorporation of the music video sequence into narrative cinema, a development led by Hollywood, and one which has allowed even greater scope for visual pyrotechnics, as manifest in the films of music video alumnus David Fincher (*Seven* [1995], *The Fight Club* [1999]). Diane's bedroom wall features a multi-panel, multicoloured lithograph of herself, mimicking Warhol's portraits of Marilyn and Elvis. The design of the title credit shot recalls Barnett Newman's 'zip' paintings. Begbie likens himself to Paul Newman in *The Hustler* (Robert Rossen, 1961); Renton reads a biography of Montgomery Clift. Sick Boy and Renton impersonate and celebrate Sean Connery-as-James Bond, the perfect symbol of internationalised celebrity culture. Sick Boy may be obsessed by Connery as a Scot, but he is a Scot most famous for an upper-class English character in a highly Americanised series of action pictures – not so very different from the Americanised Australian susperstar, Mel Gibson, playing the role of a militant Scots nationalist in another very successful Scottish film (or at least, a film about Scotland) released in the same year as *Trainspotting*, *Braveheart* (Mel Gibson, 1996).[13]

In playing up the American and international elements of the film, though, we must not lose sight of the local, regional and national cultural traditions which inform the film; it is the call and response between the regional and 'Hollywood International' that is so seductive. The national specificity of the film is evident in its title – there was much bemused debate over the meaning of 'trainspotting' outside of the UK. The regional and class specificity of the film is immediately apparent from the distinctive accent of the voice-over. The regionalism of voice here is, perhaps, less emphatic than it is in Welsh's novel, in which the phonetic rendering of local dialectic obliges the reader to sound each syllable in the mind's ear ('Yiv goat tae huv fuckin brains tae be a fuckin judge. S no iviry cunt thit kin dae that fuckin joab')[14]. Much – though not all – of the novel is written in this mode; so integral is this idiom that the American edition of the novel provides a glossary including entries for 'biscuit-ersed', 'hotchin', 'radge' and so forth.

There is, however, something of a paradox in the use of the written vernacular. It is clearly intended as a strategy of democratisation and enfranchisement, insofar as it makes the 'debased' language of a regional, working-class dialect the basis of literary narration; Kelman in particular is fiercely committed to the radical, liberatory potential of the idiom, denouncing the very use of words like 'vernacular' as ceding too much authority to standard English as an official language. The problem is that regional dialects exist almost wholly as spoken languages; when written, they may not enfranchise the speakers of that dialect as much as alienate them, as Rankin has noted: 'I loved James Kelman's first novel and took it home to my father but he said he couldn't read it because it wasn't in English. My dad is from the same working-class linguistic community as Kelman writes about. If he couldn't read it but half of Hampstead was lapping it up, that to me was a huge failure.'[15] The very same device can be appreciated for its startling, defamiliarising quality – breaking up the patterns of more familiar literary idioms, soliciting an awareness of the precise aural characteristics of an accent – and depreciated for its exclusivity. The reality for most members of minority, post-colonial cultures is that they occupy (at least) two linguistic worlds – a spoken world based on a local dialectic or language, and a written world in which an official language, or official dialectic, holds sway as the *lingua franca*. A literary movement committed to the use of regional dialect cannot change this situation overnight, and so whatever its intentions, is apt to be perceived as 'elitist' as any other form of literary innovation.

The film adopts the vernacular language of the novel, but there is a crucial transformation in its use. While the accents in general are specific enough to be recognisable as Edinburghian rather than Glaswegian or generically Scots, portions of the voice-over were re-recorded for the American release, slowing its delivery and slightly dissipating the intensity of the dialect. The intensity of the novel's 'obscene' language is also somewhat diminished (the word 'cunt', virtually a conjunction in the sociolect of the working-class youths in the novel, is considerably less pervasive in the film.) The first club scene in the film jokingly plays up the likely incomprehensibility of the working-class Scots accent to many audiences by setting the dialogue against a wall of disco music and providing subtitles for this scene even in the British release print of the film. More fundamentally, however, the film 'returns' the dialect to the domain of spoken language, in the form of dialogue and voice-over. Where written language appears in the form of subtitles (in the club scene), it does so precisely in the spirit of Rankin's remark: by accepting standard written English as standard, the 'strangeness' of the regional dialect is heightened and yet refamiliarised through translation. (*Lock, Stock and Two Smoking Barrels* appropriates this comic device, subtitling extended dialogue exchanges in both Cockney and Caribbean English.)

But what of the 'visual language' of the film? Does the film attempt to find an equivalent for the novel's written vernacular? Film-making does not involve a language in any but the loosest, most metaphorical sense; but to the extent that one could talk about a 'visual vernacular', it would perhaps be the rough 'n' ready style we associate with cinéma vérité, home movie footage and the video diary. But there is hardly a trace of this 'lo-fi' style in *Trainspotting*. Rather, the film adopts a highly crafted, stylised mode as its base currency, which nevertheless facilitates comprehension by sticking to familiar and 'legible' narrative conventions. In a striking echo of Rankin's sentiments about Kelman, Hodge has said of the film that it was not made only for 'the makers and their small coterie of Islington admirers'.[16] Insofar as we can make a comparison between novel and film in this regard, the film sticks pretty well to 'standard narrative filmese', albeit 'written' with some decorative, cursive aplomb.

Aside from verbal dialect, *Trainspotting* carefully displays national and regional fashions in dress-style and drug-taking (as the story moves into the 1990s, Ecstasy becomes more prominent); pub culture and beer drinking; traditional British breakfasts (a big close-up of fried egg, baked beans, bacon and sausage which nauseates the hungover Spud); and, notwithstanding any of my earlier comments, shifts in British musical fashion (from 1980s new wave to 1990s acid house and Britpop). The film also stresses the British national obsession – especially strong in the 1990s – with football, one which increasingly straddles class lines. A major motif in the novel is the local rivalry between Heart of Midlothian and

Drug-dazed and football-stunned

Hibernian – teams far less well-known outside of Scotland than the Glasgow clubs, Celtic and Rangers. While no mention is made of this rivalry in the film's dialogue, the production design scatters Hibs iconography through the film, beginning with the green-and-white shirts worn by Begbie and Renton in the opening five-a-side game. Soccer is a passion so strong in the film that even sexual experience is understood by analogy with it. Indeed, the footballing motif is interwoven with both sex and heroin. Renton switches a tape of Tommy and his girlfriend having sex with Tommy's '100 Great Goals' tape, and later enjoys a drug-addled viewing of the former; while in the opening montage, a hit of smoked heroin is rendered by the smack of a football on Renton's forehead, followed by crosscut, graphic mirror-images of Renton collapsing to the left and right of the screen, drug-dazed and football-stunned.

Thus, though less emphatic than in the novel, *Trainspotting*'s regional, class and subcultural markers are still to the fore. The film's strategy here is a recognisable one, even if it is executed here with unusual panache: by playing up the peculiarities of local culture, it addresses not only local but international audiences as well, for the international marketability of an art film like *Trainspotting* depends to a large degree on the 'exoticism' of its regional and local character. In effect, the film conjoins these local elements with American allusions and an international style. This can be contrasted with two alternative stategies. On the one hand, there are rare

films like *Hero* (Barney Platts-Mills, 1982), the first feature film shot in Gaelic, which make few concessions to an international audience. On the other hand, there is the overtly transatlantic strategy embodied by *Four Weddings and a Funeral* (Mike Newell, 1994) and its two successors, as well as the Boyle, Hodge, Macdonald projects which followed *Trainspotting*, *A Life Less Ordinary* (1997) and *The Beach* (2000). Although all of

Gallivant

these films feature aspects of British national and regional culture, they all also pander directly to the American market through the casting of major American stars such as Andie MacDowell, Julia Roberts, Renee Zellweger, Cameron Diaz, Holly Hunter and Leonardo DiCaprio.

Much of what I've said so far concerns the dialectic between a particular strain of Scots, working-class culture and Hollywood International; but enough has also been said to indicate that there are at least two other cultural fault lines running through the film. The first is that between Scottish and English culture, a subject particularly acute in the 1990s in the light of debates around, and the attainment of, devolution. The second schism is that between what has rapidly coalesced as 'traditional' heritage culture, and a more sceptical and ironic practice which both appeals to notions of cultural heritage while also mocking them for their anodyne character, their 'cultural racism'[17] or their downright falsity. An early instance of this counter-tradition was *The Ploughman's Lunch* (Richard Eyre, 1983), in which the eponymous salad is revealed to be nothing more than an invention of modern marketing, part of the fabrication of Olde England. As this example suggests, 'ironic heritage' culture is something shared by England and Scotland, and indeed any culture which has developed a heritage industry; an industry, that is, based on selling a prettified, nostalgic image of its host culture as a tourist commodity. We might label this alternative (anti) tradition 'garbage culture', given its central aim of rubbishing heritage culture, often through an insistent focus on the run-down and the clapped-out, on sites of destitution and poverty. Key examples include the blasted landscape of post-imperial decay distilled in Derek Jarman's *The Last of England* (1987), and less portentously, the obscure, low-rent seaside locations affectionately gathered up in Andrew Kötting's *Gallivant* (1997) around the British Isles.

These two fault lines – Scotland/England, heritage/garbage – cross one another in a crucial scene in which Renton and Tommy exchange views on the question of Scots nationalism:

TOMMY [gesturing at the stark landscape around him]: Doesn't it make you proud to be Scottish?
RENTON: It's shite being Scottish. We're the lowest of the low; the scum of the fuckin' earth. The most wretched, miserable, servile,

> pathetic trash that was ever shat in civilisation. Some people hate the
> English – I don't, they're just wankers. We on the other hand are
> colonised by wankers; can't even find a decent culture to be
> colonised by. We're ruled by effete arseholes; it's a shite state of
> affairs to be in, Tommy, and all the fresh air in the world won't make
> any fuckin' difference.

The scene manages to have its cake and eat it on both fronts. While
dismissing the English as a bunch of wankers, it takes a cynical, jaundiced
view of Scottish nationalism befitting the egoistic, drop-out anti-heroes
that the film centres upon (a point of overlap with *Shallow Grave*).
Similarly, while working in a wee dram of traditional Scottish landscape,
Tommy's desire to take a walk in the hills is dismissed as 'not natural' by
Spud, and precipitates Renton's splenetic tirade. And while we do glimpse
some of Edinburgh's grand sights, like Princes Street, as Renton and co.
are pursued through the city centre, the film concentrates on the un-
heritage Scotland of Leith, with its dilapidated council estates, threadbare
flats and appalling toilets.

But it is not only 'Scottishness' and Scottish heritage imagery that are
mocked. When Renton moves to London later in the film, the capital is
introduced by a satiric montage sequence featuring many of London's most
famous icons, including Big Ben, Trafalgar Square and its pigeons, Carnaby
St, the Lloyds Bank building and the City, a black steel-drum player in
Notting Hill, Tower Bridge, ice-cream licking tourists, and a shot of the
Pearly King and Queen smiling and waving from a red London bus. Not only
is the image of tourist-friendly London gently sent up by shots of friendly
policemen and smiling doormen, but Renton lands a job in the
quintessentially 1980s' business of estate agency, selling overpriced,
misdescribed Victorian conversions to yuppies ('this was boom town, where
any fool could make cash from chaos, and plenty did'). Nevertheless, most
of the action in this first London interlude occurs in Renton's cramped
apartment. Once Begbie and Sick Boy arrive, this space comes to resemble
more and more the decrepit hovels they inhabited in Edinburgh. Heritage is
once again overwhelmed and undercut by its doppelgänger, garbage.

3 The City's Ripped Backsides

A few moments before the exchange between Tommy and Renton over the nature of Scottish identity, there is a shot which is as startling as anything in *Trainspotting*, though it is not a shot involving a needle or faeces, nor is it one which anyone would be likely to regard as emblematic of the film or the world it depicts. It is a panoramic shot of the Scottish highlands, the torsos of Renton, Spud, Sick Boy and Tommy visible in the foreground. This shot comes as something of a shock for several reasons. First, the cut from the preceding shot – a long shot of the four characters standing in line on a railway platform – moves through 180 degrees, so that the visual field of the panoramic shot is entirely different from that of the first shot. More fundamental to the shock is the strong contrast between the two shots in terms of the nature and scale of the landscape they put before us. While the first shot appears to place the characters in a familiar urban setting, the second shot shows the gang dwarfed by the

Awayday

vast, denuded landscape of the Pentland hills. The first shot is composed so that the rural location of the train station at which they alight is obscured from us. Until the cut occurs, we take them to be in the urban space that otherwise defines the film.[18] The highland landscape revealed in the second shot is thus a kind of negative of the environment in which almost all of the action takes place. What are the constituents of city life here? What kind of Edinburgh are we shown?

The film is concerned almost wholly with urban working-class culture and working-class spaces – housing schemes, pubs, betting shops and the like – though there are some important exceptions: Diane's parents' flat, a spacious Georgian conversion recalling the main setting in *Shallow Grave*; Edinburgh's old city centre; the world of London real estate briefly inhabited by Renton; the London location of the drug deal, one of those places that seems at once well-heeled and seedy. Although the milieu depicted by *Trainspotting* is working-class, however, it is not a working one – it is, rather, a world dominated by leisure. This is established at the outset, as the opening montage crosscuts between a game of five-a-side soccer and various heroin-related activities. The only 'work' evident here is whatever it takes to acquire a supply of the drug. This is a world in which the traditional prospects and rewards associated with work are so remote, and in any case unappealing, that the decision 'to choose something' other than 'life' – junk – is presented as a rational one (in spite of Renton's disingenuous claim that 'there are no reasons' for choosing heroin).

Trainspotting is thus no lament for the loss of traditional (male) working-class existence. In this respect the film contrasts with that vein of contemporary British cinema in which the collapse of traditional industries leads to a crippling loss of self-esteem on the part of the now unemployed male labour force. In *Trainspotting*, work is simply anathema; think of Spud's wacked-out efforts to sabotage his job interview, in which he does just enough to appear to want (but not deserve or be capable of undertaking) the job. Or less obviously, consider Renton's father. In another film, he might have been presented as the working foil to Renton, salt-of-the-earth father to ne'er-do-well son. Alternatively, like many of the adult male characters in *The Full Monty*, *Billy Elliot* and *Raining Stones*, he might have been presented as unemployed, out of sorts, breaking down. But while Renton's father manifests a sturdy grumpiness familiar from other representations of working-class men, *Trainspotting* just isn't interested in his working life; it's not even clear whether he's in work. Rather, the film stresses the banality of what (we assume) a life of work has afforded Renton's parents: 'compact disc players and electrical tin openers … mind-numbing, spirit-crushing game shows', and the rest. Renton's father's life, like Renton's, is dominated by consumption rather than production; and *Trainspotting* is at least as concerned with the spiritual poverty of such consumption as it is with material poverty.

The real locus of the film is thus not traditional working-class culture – which rather forms the distant horizon to the action – but the drug underworld inhabited by Renton and his cohorts. The gang occupy a social space in which the underclass (the long-term or permanently unemployed, marooned by the collapse of traditional industry and the flight of capital) meets the counterculture (the tradition of conscious dissent from the values and lifestyle represented by modern consumer capitalism). As we know from the opening voice-over, the contempt of the counterculture for the ethos and rewards of mainstream society is present here; but it coexists with a deep pessimism about the prospects for anything better. In *La Haine* (Mathieu Kassovitz, 1995), another film from the mid-1990s which takes as its focus disaffected, unemployed youth stranded on a housing estate, there is at least the prospect of collective social rebellion: the film opens with footage of a riot, accompanied by The Wailers' protest song, 'Burnin' and Lootin'. By contrast, far from railing against the conditions of their post-industrial environment, the characters in *Trainspotting* have adapted to it. Indeed in certain respects the group mirrors, rather than opposes, the strident individualism of Thatcherite neo-conservatism.

Concretely, the drug underworld is defined not only by the spaces claimed and reclaimed by its inhabitants – the deserted netherspaces of condemned council flats, squats and motorway underpasses – but also, by extension, more familiar public spaces as the underworld moves through them. These are the ordinary flats and streets which the junkie-criminal-drop out fraternity temporarily invade and infect, as when, at the very beginning of the film, the fleeing Renton runs into the path of a car driving through the old city. The opening of the film stresses Renton's experience of the city centre as a fun house; but when the chase is re-run we get to see the frightened response of the man in the car to Renton's manic glee, in a

Deserted netherspaces

Renton's manic smile

sequence which also shows the gang preying on city centre shops, doctor's offices, old people's homes and that hapless tourist visiting the Edinburgh Festival.

And what of drug consumption itself? *Trainspotting* is only interested in a very particular social world, in which drug *consumption* is central (the film does not attempt to track the passage of drugs through every phase of production, distribution and use, in the manner of *Traffic* [Steven Soderbergh, 2000]). One of the more remarkable things about the film is its complex depiction of heroin use, which picks a path between the traps of didacticism, the glamour of heroin chic, and its inverse, the fetishisation of suffering. What's more, it manages to do this without seeming calculatedly 'balanced'. While setting drug use in a moral context, the film avoids the cant and moralising reductiveness of so much public discourse on the phenomenon; it puts drug use in a social and personal context, rather than abstracting it as simply 'wrong' (or, for that matter, 'right'). *Trainspotting* acknowledges that drugs are (in certain circumstances, for a certain duration) a source of intense pleasure – that drugs can be, as Welsh puts it, 'life enhancers'.[19]

The film tells a story in which the motivations for taking heroin, the pleasures it delivers, and the costs that addiction exacts are bound together, though not in a deterministic or uniform way: some passengers, like Renton, take the trip and survive, even thrive, while others are not so lucky. The bliss of heroin – and the alternative emotional thrills of other drugs – are shown unambiguously and unapologetically. Equally, the film is unflinching in its rendering of the degradations and risks of heroin use. These include abuse of the body (one shot shows Allison injecting Swanney somewhere in the groin;[20] a giant close-up of the interior of Renton's syringe emphasises the contaminants in the heroin; a later sequence expresses the agonies of withdrawal); the humiliation of helplessness (Renton and Spud are both shown insensate at points); the sacrifice of friendship (Renton sets Tommy out on the road to addiction); and the loss of life (the death of Allison's baby and, indirectly, Tommy). Much of the force of the 'Perfect Day' sequence derives from its simultaneous rendering of the purposes and pleasures of heroin use ('problems all left alone … you made me forget myself/I thought I was someone else/someone good … ') along with its pitfalls ('you're going to reap just what you sowed').

The rationality of heroin addiction is established not only by the conjunction of unemployment, material penury and hopelessness, but also licensed by the chemical dependency of society as a whole: just about *everyone* is on some drug or other, whether it be Renton's heroin, Begbie's alchohol, Renton's mother's valium (and even, to stretch the logic of the film only a little, Begbie's adrenalin-soaked, testosterone-driven fighting, and Tommy's sexually derived endorphins). The goal of the use of all of these drugs and elixirs is sensuous intoxication. While the film rejects the idea that sobriety is the only desirable state of human existence, it does not represent drugs as a gateway to enlightenment, to a superior or deeper insight into the nature of reality. Drugs are not the 'doors of perception' here, but rather an existential anaesthetic (as the novel puts it in one chapter title: 'Scotland Takes Drugs in Psychic Defence').

Unemployment, deprivation, poverty, misery, drugs – these are the familiar dramatic constituents of the long-standing tradition of British realist film-making. This tradition conjures up an equally recognisable *mise en scène* – of domestic squalor, cramped tenements, ruined council estates, industrial wastelands set against unyielding expanses of grey cloud; the city's ripped backsides, a world away from the grandeur of the imperial city centres.[21] Such locations are usually shot in a way which emphasises the aesthetic, and by extension spiritual, ugliness of them – whether through the functional plainness of Ken Loach, or the painfully jagged, invasively intimate style of Gary Oldman's *Nil by Mouth* (1997), a style which reveals the ugliest aspect of the underclass milieu with unforgiving candour, like a harsh fluorescent light exposing every pore and blemish in a face. This *mise en scène* is as fundamental to British realism as the suburb is to Hollywood melodrama; largely excluded by heritage culture, it is the well-spring of garbage culture. In the 1990s, many films in the already sombre tradition of British realism have taken on a particularly grim and desperate air, arising from the loss of conviction in both the Labour party and more radical socialist alternatives, which hitherto provided sources of hope. Consider Lynne Ramsey's *Ratcatcher* (1999), set on a Glasgow housing estate in the 1970s during a strike by local council workers. The estate backs onto a disused canal, in which a boy drowns within the first few minutes of the film; as the film progresses and the strike continues, the rubbish bags pile up, a feast for the local rats, compounding the atmosphere of decay and disease.

Trainspotting treats this landscape very differently. For one thing, as we've already seen, the typical locations of the realist *mise en scène* are broken up by glimpses of other worlds, and forays into other spaces: the countryside, the city centre, Diane's flat, booming London. There is also the promise –or fantasy – of escape to a more exotic location, in the form of a tropical motif in the film. This is first manifest in the infamous toilet sequence, in which Renton plunges into a filthy bowl, but emerges in a lagoon coruscating with sunlight, from which he retrieves his much-prized suppositories. The motif appears again in Spud's interview, in the form of a brightly coloured mural on the wall, depicting a stereotypical tropical idyll – golden sand, turquoise sea, palm trees (see p. 80). (Given Spud's drugged state of mind, it remains a question whether this image is on the wall or in his mind – but either way it exists as a fantasy, a fantasy of a warm, light-filled place.) The very same image then shows up on Renton's

T-shirt in London. We might compare the function of this motif with the pictures of far-flung locations (Rome, Madrid) in James Mason's midwestern house in *Bigger Than Life* (Nicholas Ray, 1956). In each case, the claustrophobic daily environment of the main characters is set against the possibility and the fragile hope of something richer.

Imagery of escape interwoven into the fabric of the realist *mise en scène* is not unique to *Trainspotting*. *Ratcatcher* contains a scene in which a pet mouse is cruelly attached to a balloon, which then floats off, irretrievably; but the viciousness of this act – cruel not only towards the mouse, but towards the young boy who is its affectionate owner – is mitigated as the mouse is seen, fantastically, to drift moonward, out of the earth's atmosphere altogether. Another motif shows the film's protagonist discovering a complex of new houses being built on the rural fringes of Glasgow, and subsequently imagining (against all the odds) that his family will move from the vermin-infested slum in which they live to this clean, bright, new place.

What *is* unique to *Trainspotting*, however – unique at least within the context of British realist film-making – is the redemption of material impoverishment through aesthetic transformation. The film depicts poverty realistically, but in a way that encompasses possibilities of escape as well as stories of entrapment. Moreover, *Trainspotting* exploits the aesthetics of film (set design, lighting, visual composition, musical scoring, and so forth) to draw a kind of vitality from grinding poverty. This is not a betrayal of reality, but an insistence that destitution need not stifle all imagination and will, mirroring the youthful defiance of the central characters. This redemptive stance is one that imbues the film as a whole – we have already seen it, for example, in the stylised blocking of the four characters as they stand, in silhouette, on the rural train platform. It is present again in the saturated colours which emanate from Swanney's pad, like the glowing, electric blue which jumps out from the screen at the beginning of the sequence in which the baby is found dead; or again in the quasi-musical choreography which characterises the meeting between Renton and Sick Boy in the park, the two of them entering the shot symmetrically and in synchrony. Two more extended examples of such aesthetic redemption will serve to describe the phenomenon more fully.

The title shot of the film – an abstract image of vertical black stripes moving horizontally over one another, like an animated Op Art painting – precedes the first shot of Renton's flat. What is striking about this shot of Renton's flat is that it echoes many of the compositional features of the title shot. The image is framed frontally, so that the composition is dominated by vertical and horizontal lines. The chief objects within the shot are laid out to echo these lines – Renton's table, for example, is pushed flat against the wall the camera faces, rather than being set at an eccentric angle. More subtly, the vertical motif established by the title shot is sustained by both the tablecloth and the paint on the wall, both of which exhibit a design based on vertical stripes. In another words, although in the transition from the title shot to the establishing shot of Renton's flat we have moved from an abstract image to a depiction of a space within the story – and a typically drab one at that – this space is shown to us in an overtly formalised fashion, which invests it with an aesthetic verve absent from standard realist *mise en scène*.

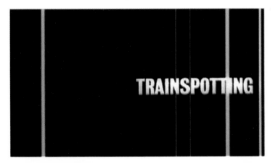

Title shot

Renton's flat

The same is true of the shot in which Renton walks by a block of flats, on his way to the betting shop. The composition is again frontal, with the facing wall of the block of flats forming another quasi-abstract, rectilinear composition, this time a set of squares (the windows) filled with a variety of textures and colours (various blinds and curtains). Renton moves along a line parallel with the facing wall, reinforcing the formalised quality of the composition, up until the moment that he crumples with intestinal pain. This, of course, reminds us of where we are, and what is happening, and the action in the betting shop toilet will rub our noses in the realities of this environment. But recall that the toilet scene is followed by Renton's dive into the fantastic lagoon, and even as he staggers through the betting shop on the way to the toilet, Renton speaks of a 'pristine convenience' which he sees in his mind's eye. The unalloyed awfulness of poverty is thus continuously off-set by the processes of imaginative and aesthetic transformation. Such transformation does not amount to an escapist sugaring-of-the-pill, because the unpalatable realities of the world are still

The heroin wears off

evident; but neither does it pretend to effect, or substitute for, the actual elimination of these realities. Rather, the claim of aesthetic redemption is, precisely and modestly, an aesthetic one; that it is a more subtle, more inclusive – one might say more realistic, if this didn't immediately conjure paradox – mode of representation than either conventional social realism or pure escapism.[22]

4 Like Friends

Trainspotting is perhaps most renowned for its head-on representation of things underground and forbidden, and for its style – its confident swagger as a piece of film-making. But at its core, *Trainspotting* tells a highly emotive story dwelling on some very traditional themes: childhood, friendship, loyalty – and the messy business of leaving all of these behind. And at the heart of this story lies a love triangle – one that has little or nothing to do, however, with the women in the film, like Renton's sometime girlfriend Diane.[23] This triangle is formed instead by three pivotal members of the gang: Renton, Spud and Begbie. As the story unfolds, the central emotional questions of friendship and loyalty are most keenly dramatised through this central trio.

Begbie makes his first major appearance some fifteen minutes into the film, holding court in a pub with the entire circle of friends (the gang and their girlfriends) gathered around him as he relates a (false) story building up his hard-man legend and pool prowess. Begbie appears at the centre of the group, with the eyes and smiling faces of the others fixed attentively on him in admiration. That's the way Begbie sees it – but he is as self-deceived as the story he tells is bogus. Begbie's embattled psychology, jittery paranoia and constant need to dominate others betray a deep sense of insecurity.

Begbie's grip on his friends arises out of a combination of misplaced, almost pathological, loyalty to him, supported by a kind of ideology of absolute friendship ('he's a mate, so what can you do'), along with his ability to browbeat and physically intimidate just about anyone he encounters, including his own associates. The true nature of the relationship between Begbie and the rest emerges first from small, revelatory gestures scattered among the ritual, 'attentive' smiles: brief refusals to meet Begbie's eye and give assent to his braggadocio, glances away from the group, exasperated sighs qualifying the performance of Friday-night jollity. And then, as the film freezes on Begbie, the narration shifts sideways and forwards, to Tommy's retelling of Begbie's pool story (to Renton, some time later in Tommy's flat). Far from clearing the table with his potting expertise, Begbie plays so badly – labouring under a bad hangover – that he rips the cloth on the pool table. Physically venting his frustration on a pub customer, when Tommy tries to intervene Begbie turns on him, knife drawn. This is the first clear sign that Begbie's violence is directed not only at enemies and bystanders, but also towards his friends. As we will see later, if the relationship between Begbie and Renton is a spousal one, it is also a deeply abusive one.

The film freezes on Begbie as he casually tosses a beer glass from the first floor of the pub – where the group are drinking – onto the unsuspecting throng down below, an act which provokes the fight he is seeking: 'Begbie didn't do drugs … – he just did people; his own sensory addiction.' A woman is badly cut by the flying glass; Begbie plays the part of indignant male protector; the mêlée ensues. Begbie's psychotic attachment to violence might be the dramatic focus of the sequence, but the associated moral culpability of his friends is a part of the picture too: the pusillanimous and two-faced way in which they fawn on Begbie; and their detachment from the havoc Begbie creates, as they watch the fight from the first floor, for all the world as if watching from the circle seats in a theatre.

The ethical shortcomings of the group have already been set up by Renton's voice-over commentary, earlier in the sequence. As Tommy relates his version of the story, Renton quietly steals the tape containing footage of Tommy and his girlfriend Lizzy having sex – an act which will ultimately have catastrophic results for Tommy. But even here, where it seems like nothing more than a mean-spirited prank on a friend, the evil of the act seems amplified by Renton's failure to register any level of wrongdoing at all (along with the fact that he is doing it to Tommy, who is described by Renton as the one really decent member of the gang). Later, watching the tape with Sick Boy, Renton's voice-over notes that 'something important was missing'; but while we've been led to recognise that it is a sense (*any* sense) of ethical responsibility that is missing, all Renton has in mind is sex – like heroin and fighting, another form of sensory pleasure and escape. It's important to note here the split between Renton the character, embodied in the scenes, and Renton, the voice-over narrator. While Renton the character is often represented – especially early in the story – as myopic, Renton the narrator shows much greater awareness and sensitivity on a number of levels, and the often ironic contrast between the two fundamentally shapes the stance we take towards Renton and the other characters.

Later in the film, when Renton has come off heroin for the second time, he is visited by Diane. She is instrumental in making Renton see that he has to escape the oppressive circle of male friends and the stagnant life they represent. So he moves to London. She writes to him and provides a brief report on his erstwhile chums: Sick Boy has moved into pimping; Spud, now out of prison, apparently picks up his inebriated existence from where he left off; and Begbie is wanted for armed theft of a jewellery store. But no sooner has Renton read the letter than Begbie is ringing the doorbell of his London flat; leaving his old friends behind proves to be much more difficult than he had anticipated. Begbie moves in, acting like a domineering spouse (even as Renton performs the role of breadwinner), sending Renton out to fetch cigarettes, beer and place bets, overrunning the flat with his presence and habits. The song by Pulp ('Mile End') which accompanies the sequence stresses the slum-like squalor that evolves in Begbie's presence, all through the screen of a bouncing bittersweet melody, like a forced smile: 'it smelt as if someone had died/the living room was full of flies ... the lift is always full of piss/the fifth floor landing smells of fish.' Diane threatens to break the bonds of male camaraderie holding Renton in his old position, but we are forcefully reminded of the nature and power of these ties by Begbie's rapid reappearance, and the presumptive manner in which he immediately asserts his dominance over Renton.[24]

Of course, nothing would horrify Begbie more than to hear his relationship with Renton described in these terms. Begbie's unreconstructed attitudes towards sexuality are capped by his encounter at the rave. Following a win on the horses, Begbie and Renton celebrate with a night out, but Begbie discovers that the woman he thinks he's picked up is in fact a male transvestite. Begbie is thus faced with his *Crying Game* moment. Traumatised by this affront to his sense of the sexual order of things, he reacts violently when Renton ribs him about his unexpected discovery, stabbing his knife into the wall just below Renton's crotch and threatening to 'cut' him up. Begbie's strident homosociality (that is, commitment to male camaraderie) is thus shown to be contingent upon an equally virulent homophobia. The film provides no support, however, for the psychoanalytic conceit that homosociality, and the homophobia that so often comes with it, is really a form of repressed homosexuality. The one moment in which there is any evidence of erotic desire among the gang members occurs near the beginning of the film, when Spud, fresh from shooting up, kisses an initially disconcerted Sick Boy on the mouth. A few moments later Swanney, also high, playfully nuzzles and bites Sick Boy like an affectionate dog. But this is less about repressed homoeroticism than – to put it in Freudian terms – the polymorphous sensuality produced by heroin, which transcends sexual activity *tout court*: in the same scene, Allison lets Sick Boy know that a heroin high 'beats any meat injection'.

The rave is the last occasion – bar one – when we see Renton seeming to enjoy the company of any of the members of the gang. Following Begbie's attack, Sick Boy arrives, and the pattern of presumption, exploitation and betrayal by these 'friends' escalates: Sick Boy sells Renton's TV, eats his food and ominously suggests that a good price could be obtained for Renton's passport, should he wish to sell it (Renton immediately places it in a railway station locker). After Tommy's funeral, Sick Boy and Begbie coerce him into using his savings to finance the skag deal – they know he has the money because while in London they made it their business to read his bank statements – and testing the heroin. As far as Begbie and Sick Boy are concerned, Renton has no autonomy; whatever Renton possesses, the gang owns – at least when it suits them. The full force of Renton's earlier, anxious statement, when coming off heroin for the first time, comes home at this point: 'I would have to mix with my friends again – in a state of full consciousness.'

As we gradually come to understand, there is little pleasure and positive commitment left in the gang, especially as far as Renton is concerned. But there is an exceptional moment when they are brought together in sorrow, following Tommy's death. Sitting in the familiar local pub on the housing scheme, Spud sings 'Two Little Boys', unaccompanied and uninterrupted by Begbie's outbursts or Sick Boy's selfish quips. Even Renton's sardonic voice-over falls silent during this lament for the loss and destruction of childhood friendship by adult allegiances. The emotional force of the scene – the most overtly sentimental in the film, without a trace of irony – depends to a great extent on a shift away from the pace and style which characterises most of the film. The action is depicted in a single long shot, sustained for the duration of the song; nobody moves or gestures as Spud sings and the camera tracks slowly towards him. The style of the song is important too in this change of narrational temper: while most pieces of music in the film drive the action forward with heavily accented rhythms, and the aural plenitude available to orchestral or pop underscoring, the sound of a lone, mournful voice singing a children's ballad stops the film dead in its tracks. This is the still centre of a film which, for the most part, can't stop moving.

As an aside, it is worth considering how this scene compares with the chapter from the novel ('Memories of Matty') on which it is based. In his introduction to the screenplay of *Trainspotting*, Hodge notes that this is his favourite chapter in Welsh's novel; but that, along with many other incidents and characters, most of the dramatic material from the chapter had to be left out of the adaptation. He goes on: 'All that survives … is Spud's attention to Australian pop culture after Tommy's funeral, but even that moment is left unexplained in the forward rush of screen time. For a more complete understanding of that scene and all others, please refer to the book.'[25] Albeit with tongue lodged firmly in cheek, Hodge drastically underplays the extent of the transformation, treating it as simply a loss of detail, rather than a complete change of emphasis and tone. Far from being simply a jokey token of the kitsch Australian pop culture associated with Matty in the novel, 'Two Little Boys' evokes startling pathos when sung by Spud in the film.

Spud's doleful air is sustained into the subsequent scene when Sick Boy proposes the heroin deal. For a second Renton is amazed that the rest of them can even be contemplating such an idea in the wake of Tommy's death from AIDS. (This is the moment to spell out Renton's role in the causal chain leading to Tommy's demise: Renton steals the tape of Lizzy and Tommy having sex, and this becomes a major factor in the couple's break-up; despondent, Tommy approaches Renton for heroin; at first diffident, Renton readily supplies when Tommy waves some money at him, the Pavlovian reflex of the junkie; Tommy becomes an addict and contracts HIV through an infected needle; he dies an isolated, miserable death from toxoplasmosis.) Renton appeals to Spud to introduce some sense into the discussion. 'I just want the money, Mark,' Spud responds. Notably, for the first and only time in the film, Renton is addressed by one of his male friends by his first name, rather than as 'Rents', 'Rentboy' or 'Catboy' (Spud's nickname for him). While Begbie and Sick Boy seem to press on heedless with the same old routines, Spud now seems to be motivated by sheer desperation. In his own way, like Renton, if not with the same sense of calculation or will, Spud's commitment to the gang is beginning to wither away.

The single remaining moment of joy for the gang comes when the heroin deal has been successfully – give or take a few thousand pounds – pulled off: 'just for a moment it felt really good, like we were all in it together – like friends.' As soon as we see them in (yet another) pub after the deal, light-hearted but meaningful banter about trust and distrust among the four of them begins. They even briefly squabble over whose round is next. All of this leads up to another episode of Begbiean violence, mirroring the first such scene in the film, involving the thrown beer glass. This time Begbie – doubtless agitated by the fact that he was compelled to

The gang celebrate

buy a round of drinks for his mates – bumps into a local in the pub, deliberately spilling beer over himself. Contriving another violent showdown, Begbie verbally abuses the unfortunate customer, smashing a glass in his face the moment he tells Begbie, quite justifiably, to 'fuck off '. The shot preceding the one in which Begbie launches the beer glass into the man's face shows the other pints of beer that Begbie had been holding smashing on the ground, the shattered glass and liquid adumbrating the spectacle of blood, beating and ripped flesh about to ensue. Sick Boy remonstrates with Begbie; Spud tries to restrain him, and for his pains Begbie slices Spud's hand with the ubiquitous knife, as he draws it on his now helpless, bleeding victim. For the third time – following his attacks on Tommy and Renton – one of Begbie's 'friends' becomes the object of Begbie's violence. And to confirm his status as leader and dominant

Begbie cuts Spud's hand

Renton's alienation

spouse one more time, Begbie orders Renton to bring and light him a cigarette in the midst of this scene of paralysed carnage. Taking a drag, Begbie exhales directly into Renton's face, with that characteristic mixture of intimacy and hostility reserved for his friends.

The fight, it seems, is the final spur of encouragement that Renton needs to go through with the theft of the money, an idea he floats with Spud when Begbie is getting the round in and Sick Boy is in the toilet. One shot in particular seems to represent the decisive moment of Renton's alienation from the gang: as the stand-off between Begbie, Sick Boy and Spud goes on out of focus and in the background, we see Renton in extreme close-up in the foreground, his back turned to the other members of the gang. His expression is hard to read; but this is clearly not the Renton we see in the earlier bar fight, indifferently gazing upon the suffering and mayhem caused by Begbie. If only out of self-interest, something inside Renton has snapped.

5 A Bad Person

What are we to make of Renton's act of double-crossing? In his voice-over, Renton presents himself cynically: 'a moment like that', he says of the collective exhilaration the gang experience when the deal is closed, 'can touch you deep inside – but not like £16,000.' As the movie ends, he goes on to describe himself as simply and fundamentally a 'bad person', implying that we shouldn't be taken in by any efforts he might make to excuse or exonerate himself. Do we – can we – take Renton's self-criticism at face value?

I want to argue that we do exonerate Renton, to a very large degree, and we do so in part *because* he says these things. His cynicism and self-criticism at least have the virtue of honesty. And in any case, he is too hard on himself. Given the prison-house of male bonding the film depicts, this is an act of justifiable self-liberation. Begbie's embodiment of psychotic masculinity is a sort of anti-model, which serves both to motivate and to exculpate Renton's theft of the money. Renton has tried to escape this life before, but Begbie and Sick Boy track him down and drag him back in; so there is a way in which they have brought Renton's betrayal on themselves. Moreover, the film ends not by stressing Renton's disloyalty to Sick Boy and Begbie, but his loyalty – even tenderness – towards the harmless Spud: Renton collects his passport from the locker and replaces it with a wad of banknotes, and in the final live-action shot of the film, we see Spud discovering the money left for him. Perhaps there is also an element of atonement here, for the fact that earlier in the story Spud goes down for theft and possession, while the wily Renton merely has to commit to a drugs rehabilitation programme (the judge imprisons Spud because he deems him to be 'without regret or remorse', but in reality he is simply less cunning and articulate than Renton). Is there not a faint echo here of Christian sentiment: and the last shall be first?

Well, not quite. To get a firmer grip on these questions, we need to step back and examine how the film situates us with regard to Renton – the degree to which the film invites us to root for him, criticise him or admire him. It may seem obvious that Renton is the hero of *Trainspotting*, both in the sense that he is the dramatic centre of the film, and in the sense that he is the locus of positive value. But a closer look reveals a more intricate and varied structure. The film follows and gives visual emphasis to Renton most of the time. The opening action in this sense is representative: Renton runs towards the camera in the foreground, with Spud visible behind him to the right. But the film does not stick with Renton narrowly or slavishly; consider the crosscut action involving not only Renton and Diane, but Tommy and Lizzy, and Spud and Gail, the morning after the night at the club. But still we feel the post-club action is vitally connected with Renton, thematically and causally: the other characters are his friends; like him they have spent the night, more or less successfully, in pursuit of sex; and in the case of Tommy and Lizzy, as we have seen, Renton is directly responsible for the calamitous loss of the sex tape.

But another technique is absolutely vital in creating the impression that this is Renton's story, even as the film, in visual terms, strays from him: the voice-over. The voice-over is extensive, frequently serving as a transition from one scene to another. Most importantly in this context, the voice-over binds shots and scenes which do not directly involve Renton to his perspective and experience. In the opening scene, the film fans out from Renton, visually foregrounding other members of the group during the five-a-side football game, culminating with Allison, Sick Boy, Spud and Swanney shooting up with Renton nowhere to be seen. But Renton's voice-over weaves its way through this action, so that we perceive the whole as a depiction of *his* life. And just as Renton's voice-over bookends many sequences, so it frames the film as a whole.

The opening voice-over monologue ('Choose life …') appears to nail the film's countercultural, hedonistic colours to the mast, if we take Renton to be the metaphorical as well as literal voice of the film.[26] The monologue is a classic countercultural statement in its manifesto-like form and ranting manner, as well as its corrosive appraisal of the goals, cherished objects and implicit values of ordinary consumer society. What immediately begins to take shape, partly as the 'negative' image of the mainstream culture scorned by the monologue, is an alternative value system. In examining how this is achieved, it will be useful to turn to Friedrich Nietzsche's ambition to 'transvalue' (or 'revalue') existing values. For Nietzsche, the 'slave morality' of Christianity is a morality of resentment: pride and intellectual freedom are decried as 'evils', while self-denial, shame of the body and persecution of non-believers are regarded as 'goods'. Investing its hopes in the fantasy of an all-powerful God and the afterlife, Christianity overvalues worldly abstinence and sacrifice, while undervaluing the life-affirming qualities of courage, sensuous pleasure and 'intellectual libertinage'. Nietzsche's expression of these ideas often takes the form of a passionate tirade against conventional value systems, replete with slogans and catchphrases.[27]

The opening monologue proposes a most dramatic transvaluation of conventional values. 'Life', as it is understood and lived by mainstream society, is *death* for Renton and his ilk: 'Choose life. Choose a job. Choose a career … Choose rottin' away at the end of it all …' So begins a whole system of inversions and revaluations: when Tommy suggests that the gang take a walk in the 'great outdoors' one day, Spud complains that such activities are 'not natural'; immediately following this, Renton, Spud and the aptly named Sick Boy take a 'healthy and informed decision' to go back on junk. Honesty and integrity come in for the same treatment: 'You always got the truth from Tommy – it was one of his major weaknesses.' The niceties of affluent bourgeois existence are parodied when Renton visits Swanney for a hit, Swanney playing the role of *maitre d'* to Renton's customer in a posh restaurant (a scene employing a premise similar to Peter Greenaway's *The Cook, The Thief, His Wife and Her Lover* [1989]). The orderliness and decorum of bourgeois existence are burlesqued by Renton's meticulous approach to 'relinquishing heroin', Bizet's *Carmen* reduced to the role of aural anaesthetic (complementing the valium, mouthwash and Lucozade). The role of the list in consumer culture – so important in creating a sense of material abundance and choice, and of bestowing value and desirability on the enumerated items ('Top Ten drugs …') – is subverted here by Renton's acid, rapid-fire inventory of consumer 'delights', a list which flattens value through grinding, repetitive attrition; the treadmill of consumerism. Elsewhere Christian imagery and ideas in particular are inverted and travestied: Swanney is known as the 'Mother Superior' due to the length of his 'habit', and his flat is permeated by a saturated light evocative of stained glass. Similarly, when Renton declares in court that 'with God's help I'll conquer this terrible affliction', he mocks Christian remorse and devotion.[28] Here the parallel with Nietzsche is close indeed: his final work possesses the self-explanatory title *The Anti-Christ*.

Thus, the film adheres to traditional dramatic structure – insofar as the protagonist is both likeable and admirable on the whole – but what counts as a virtue has shifted. Renton is, in part, an 'anti-hero': a hero whose heroism is derived from overturning an alternative, 'false' set of values – a hero who effects the Nietzschean transvaluation of values. What, then, are the alternative values that emerge from the invective directed against mainstream culture? The two most salient values are egoism and hedonism. To grasp the place of egoism in Renton's worldview, consider his remarks on sex and gender orientation. At the rave club, Renton envisages a future world in which the distinct sexes disappear, leaving 'just wankers'. This is put forward as a positive development – as a step beyond the rigid sexual dichotomies that Begbie insists upon. But the vision isn't of a future of anxiety-free transcendence of sexual difference, but of genderless onanists – 'wankers' – seeking to maximise their own sexual pleasure. To be precise, being a 'wanker' isn't exactly something held up by Renton as a virtue; it is rather a reality which one either recognises and lives with, or turns away from in self-deception. Recall the scene in which Renton rails against Scotland: the English are merely 'wankers' – not so bad – but the Scots are 'colonised by wankers'. Extreme egoism is embodied above all by Sick Boy; his off-hand 'why not? – I know I would' statement in the penultimate bar scene is another important moment in the chain of events leading to Renton's theft of the money and 'betrayal' of the gang. All is self-interest; better to accept this and *carpe diem*.

Enter hedonism – the prioritisation of immediate gratification over everything else. Heroin, of course, represents hedonism writ large. But this hedonism is intimately tied up with nihilism: grasping the most intense, immediate pleasures is the flip side of an utterly bleak view of the long term. Here we encounter another parallel with Nietzsche: while for Nietzsche the self-denial of Christian morality is explained by the investment of hopes in a future afterlife, so the deferral of gratification is at the heart of the junkie critique of middle-class life: 'Choose good health, low cholesterol and dental insurance. Choose fixed interest mortgage repayments.' The immediate pleasures of bodily intoxication are valued over the potential rewards of self-denial, sobriety and hard graft.[29]

The opening chase, and its reprise later in the film, neatly captures the relationship between nihilism and hedonism: the first rendering of the chase is all about exhilaration; the second rendering is not merely an expression of pessimism, but specifically about the vicious circle of dependence between nihilism and narcotics: 'pile misery upon misery, heap it up in a spoon and dissolve it with a drop of bile, then squirt it into a stinking, purulent vein and do it all over again.' In this respect, the counterculture represented by Renton and company signally lacks the grand ambition, the hope and the belief in the possibility of transformation that is an element of both Nietzsche's project of 'transvaluation' and of the classic countercultures, like those of the Beats in the 1950s and the hippies in the 1960s. Indeed, some might balk at my description of the junkie worldview given expression in *Trainspotting* as 'countercultural' for precisely this reason.

But this would be to perceive the variety of countercultural thought too narrowly. Alongside the utopian countercultural traditions exists a cynical alternative, often in the forefront of postwar youth culture. Once we understand the transvaluation of the word 'life' at work in *Trainspotting*, we can see that the use of Iggy Pop's 'Lust for Life' over the film's opening minutes reverberates with the cry of disenchanted youth across the decades: as The Who declared in 1965 in 'My Generation', 'Hope I die before I get old ...' From early rock 'n' roll to the proto-punk of Iggy and the Stooges through to 1970s punk itself, such nihilism is a crucial part of the cultural backdrop to *Trainspotting*. It is manifest in the film not only in the form of Iggy, but in Renton's cropped, undernourished look and Sick Boy's peroxide hair; Welsh himself (as Mikey Forrester) sports a yelling punk singer on his T-shirt, complete with that quintessential item of punk couture, the mohawk. Malcolm McClaren, Svengali behind the Sex Pistols, features in Sick Boy's pantheon of heroes, while the explosive and direct musical aesthetic of punk is vestigially present through the various first- and second-generation new wave bands featuring in the film's score (New Order, Pulp, Primal Scream, Blur and Elastica).

While Nietzsche's transvaluation was an attempt to transcend the compromised and life-denying character of Christian morality, there is little prospect of – or ambition for – transcendence in Renton's attack on conventional values. Indeed, so far from transcending these values, *Trainspotting* presents the junkies as, in part, simply the logical extension of aspects of mainstream society. Discussing his mother's valium, Renton notes that she is, 'in her own socially acceptable way', a drug addict. Upon his move to London, Renton finds that he fits right in to the world of real estate, the symbol *par excellence* of the Thatcherite ethos of the day: 'There was no such thing as society, and if there was, I was almost certainly not part of it.' With their parallel commitments to self-interest, greed and short-term gain, the junkies constitute a revealing mirror image of the political and economic neo-conservatism of the 1980s. Both stand in contrast to the ordinary, lower-middle-class and working-class life that we see elsewhere in the film.

Renton, however, is a more complex character than he appears to be. Almost as soon as the countercultural emphasis on self-interest, hedonism and nihilism is established, a competing value system hovers alongside it. The film is peppered with incidents where Renton is shown to be sensitive and thoughtful – certainly far more so than any of his friends. Some of these moments are dramatic outcroppings, as when Renton shows compassion towards Spud's mother in the pub; others take the form of small details, which nevertheless help to build a picture of Renton as a decent human being, at variance with the way he appears to celebrate his 'bad person' self-image. Thus, when Diane writes to Renton, she thanks him for asking her if she is pregnant, implying a concern for her well-being that need not and should not occupy him, according to his avowed beliefs. One of the most significant techniques used by the film to develop this 'double image' of Renton is the voice-over. We have already examined the way in which the voice-over creates the sense that everything is filtered through Renton's sensibility. What we now need to add is that image and voice-over, on occasion and to varying degrees, act in counterpoint to one another.

Incongruities between image and voice-over are sometimes used to create comic irony: as Renton describes his attempt to lead 'a useful and fulfilling life as a good citizen', we see him reloading an air rifle, and then consuming a milkshake. More significantly in this context, the voice-over often complicates the moral picture we have of Renton. In the scene in which the baby dies, for example, Renton is presented visually as pretty egoistic: brought to consciousness by Allison's screaming, he is startled and clearly troubled, but quickly moves to shoot up. These actions,

Parklife with Renton and
Sick Boy

however, are framed by a reflective voice-over. Responding to Spud's
weary assurance that 'everything's gonna be just fine', Renton-as-narrator
states that 'on the contrary everything was gonna be bad. Bad? I mean
everything was going to be worse than it already was ...' For perhaps the
first time in the film, Renton reverts to ordinary moral language; moral
language that has not been subverted, inverted, parodied or transvalued.
Renton-the-narrator thus reveals Renton-the-character to be at least partly
committed to a recognisable mainstream value system – one which
includes compassion for the grief-stricken – for all his apparent adherence
to egoistic nihilism. An instructive contrast can be drawn here between
Renton and his counterpart in *Naked*, Johnny (David Thewlis). Where
Renton's sensitivity to others frames or at least balances his egoism, the
emphasis is reversed in Leigh's film, Johnny's violent misogyny and cruelty
all but eradicating his occasional gestures of kindness.

Let us consider the final scene once again, then, in the light of the
complex picture of both Renton and the alternative, countercultural value

'I wished I could think of
something to say ...'

system that he at first appears to embody. As Renton leaves the gang and the film draws to a conclusion, he is delicately poised between mainstream and countercultural value systems. When Renton states 'I am a bad person', the word 'bad' points towards two sets of criteria. On the one hand, for 'bad' read 'good': Renton has had the courage and the smarts to seize the moment and break from the corrupting influence, and diminishing returns, of life in the gang. He has, finally, lifted himself out of his own particular 'herd' – not the slavish conformity to Christian values that Nietzsche targeted, but the lemming mentality imposed by membership of the gang. On the other hand, he just is *bad*, on the conventional understanding, since he has now betrayed his friends, the one group who, especially according to the ideals of male camaraderie discussed in the last section, are supposed to be exempt from the ravages of egoism.

Even on these conventional terms, however, he carries our sympathy, insofar as his actions are 'proportionate' to the injuries he has suffered at the hands of the gang. The ending of the film is thus affirmative – glowingly affirmative, with no sense that Renton really thinks that he's 'bad,' or is weighed down by guilt, as he strides over the Thames, an irrepressible smile breaking out on his face. Indeed, in dramatic terms the film's ending is comic, delivering the promise of rebirth. Renton's story also bears comparison with the *Bildungsroman*, the (originally German) novel of 'character formation'. In its traditional form, such a novel would end with the central character finding his place and integrating with society. The ending of *Trainspotting* in these terms is, once again, ambiguous. On the one hand, Renton breaks with the gang and thus with his past, and to that degree appears to be abandoning his life as a countercultural 'outsider' for something more conventional. On the other hand, he has just stolen several thousand pounds, money obtained from the sale of illegal drugs, and doesn't seem too perplexed by his actions: hardly the behaviour of a model citizen. Renton's final words evoke ironically the idea of social integration – 'I'm going to be just like you: the job, the family, the fucking big television …' – but the force of the irony is qualified by the kinship between the junkies and self-interested consumerism that the film has established. If Renton can be said to become integrated with any group at the end of the film, it is simply with the audience – the youthful, liberal, 'cool' audience whose approval the film above all seeks.

Renton moves on

Begbie is left behind

Renton's gift to Spud

No wonder Renton is smiling: he wins on all fronts, being both decent (sensitive and compassionate) and 'bad' (smart, hip and self-assertive) – that is, good and thus admirable according to both mainstream and countercultural criteria. Perhaps this is the force of the marketing description of Renton: compassionate and rebellious, hero and anti-hero, Renton is held up as 'a hero for our times'.

6 Speed of Life

After his trial for shoplifting, Renton morosely contemplates the life before him – a life without the compromising but intense pleasures of heroin, and without the compensations of community with friends or family, consolations which are unavailable to him because of his lack of faith in these institutions. Climbing onto a wall behind the pub where his evasion of a prison sentence is being celebrated, Renton balances on it for a few seconds, and then leaps off the other side – landing not in the adjoining yard, however, but in Swanney's flat, where he buys 'one last hit'. Renton's 'impossible' leap through space is emblematic of the graceful, feline dynamism of *Trainspotting* as a whole.

The most obvious signs of the film's distinctive style are its rapid speed and propulsive forward momentum – a rough cut of two hours and twenty minutes was edited down to a svelte ninety minutes – and plasticity of style. The film adopts a heightened *mise en scène* in many sequences:

Renton's magical leap

Forced perspective

consider the forced perspective and exaggerated depth in Spud's interview (see p. 80) and in Renton's bedroom; the expressionistic colour scheme in Swanney's flat (alternating blood reds and lurid greens, with some purple thrown in to complete the Francis Bacon-inspired palette); and the flat compositions in which the shapes and colours of characters and buildings are strung out laterally across the screen. A fish-eye lens warps space as Renton moves through the betting shop, distorted figures looming towards him; when he reaches the toilet itself, the film pauses for a second, freeze-framing on the closing door in order to label it –

The graphically playful montage of Renton's collapse in the opening sequence not only rapidly intercuts two separate moments, but throws in an inversion of screen direction: drug-addled Renton begins falling to the left, but lands to the right (see p. 23). Such play recurs in the short scene in which Spud and Renton drink a milkshake together: rapid-fire montage creates a jagged transition into the scene as the two of them suck the glass empty. The editing here is so fast that the screen is briefly dominated by the abstract dynamism of rapidly alternating diagonals. The final two-shot of the lads sucking pulls back quickly but briefly, creating a labile, quicksand space, an effect echoed elsewhere in the film by vertiginous shifts in shot scale and focal length from shot to shot.

Another telling indication of the style of *Trainspotting* is the displacement of the scene, strictly defined – a stretch of narrative defined by the traditional unities of time, space and action.[30] In such a scene, the action of the story moves forward seamlessly across the cuts from shot to shot, and the motivations and intentions of the characters are revealed directly through speech, gesture and movement. Diegetic sound – the speech and other sounds of the story world – dominates the sound mix; if present at all, non-diegetic, commentative music plays the role of unobtrusively underscoring the action. Such 'ordinary' scenes are the bread and butter of most films. My argument will not be that the ordinary scene is wholly absent from *Trainspotting*, but rather that where such scenes are deployed, they often exert a special emotional force.

What then takes the place of the ordinary scene in the storytelling fabric of *Trainspotting*? Broadly speaking, the film uses a variety of sequence-types which share a far greater elasticity of time and space than is characteristic of the ordinary scene. Consider the sex sequence which brings to a climax the evening spent at the Volcano club. Renton follows Diane out of the club and they go back to her flat (as it seems at the time) in a cab. But this action is not narrated to us in continuous fashion. Instead, in a manner reminiscent of the central sequence in *Sammy and Rosie Get Laid* (Stephen Frears, 1987), the film crosscuts between Diane and Renton, and the established couples, Tommy and Lizzy, Spud and Gail, as they leave the club and then arrive back at their respective homes, all of them intent on sex. (All of them except for Spud, that is, who passes out on Gail's bed.) Such parallel editing exhibits unity of time – we understand that the three sexual encounters are occurring roughly simultaneously – but no unity of action and space, as the sequence bounces us from one set of characters to another.

This is not to say that the sequence lacks cohesiveness. The intrinsic narrative parallels between the three couples are underlined by the continuous presence of the song 'Atomic', which begins as diegetic sound in the club but continues throughout the sequence, thus assuming non-diegetic status. (Even as diegetic sound, however, it performs a commentative purpose: the song begins just as Renton catches sight of Diane, for the first time, across the dance floor.) As the sequence mounts to its largely bathetic climax – two of the three sexual ventures being

'He's going all the way...he scores !'

foiled – this melding of distinct dramatic spaces through sound is taken a step further. In Tommy's flat, Lizzy has urged Tommy to put on their sex tape, so that they can watch each other have sex on TV as they have sex in the flesh. As the video starts to run, footage of the 1978 World Cup match between Scotland and Holland appears on the screen, to Tommy's consternation. A series of progressively closer shots of the TV, showing Archie Gemmill's famous weaving run and goal, are crosscut with Renton and Diane achieving orgasm, with the sound of the TV commentator (literally only present in Tommy's flat) audible throughout, setting up one of the film's more shameless moments of humour: 'what a penetrating goal!'

The kind of parallel editing in evidence here is established at the very beginning of the film, in the opening 'Lust for Life' sequence. In fact, this sequence is even more complex. It begins with Renton and company fleeing security guards in the centre of Edinburgh; the sequence then moves back and forth between Renton as he smokes heroin, five-a-side football with the gang and collective junkie activity at Swanney's place. The exact temporal relationships here are indeterminate: it's not clear at this point whether the chase follows or precedes the football game. The sequence thus establishes the everyday routines of the characters involved rather than the unique significance of the action that we see. (When we see the chase a second time, its purpose and emphasis shift, ending the phase of 'innocent' junkiedom in Renton's life, culminating as it does in his arrest. So the temporal ordering of the action is clarified, and the chase becomes a kind of turning point.)

The most intricate example of *Trainspotting*'s playful mode of storytelling, which rapidly shuttles us around in time and space, is to be found in the film's use of 'embedded' narration, in which a series of miniature stories are nested inside one another. The scene in the bar which introduces Begbie is the most sustained and elaborate example of such narration. The sequence begins with Begbie regaling the group in the pub with his story. The film gives Begbie enough rope to hang himself with – Begbie tells his phony, ego-polishing story interrupted only by a single, brief subjective shot showing him effortlessly potting a ball – but then the film freeze-frames on Begbie as he tosses the beer glass backwards, and Renton-as-narrator introduces Tommy's true version of the story. But

Renton's voice-over doesn't directly recount Tommy's story; rather, it ushers us into the new space of Tommy's flat, where we see Tommy lifting weights and telling the story to Renton, who is browsing through Tommy's video collection. Another line of action is initiated here: through a series of point-of-view shots we realise that Renton is switching a tape hand-labelled 'Tommy + Lizzy Vol. 1' with another, commercial tape entitled '100 Great Goals'.

Sandwiched in between the shots which show us what Renton is up to, however, the film inserts *another* series of retrospective shots, illustrating and embellishing the tale Tommy is relating (concerning Begbie's inept pool playing and his attack on a bystander; these shots recall, but also negate, Begbie's subjective shot earlier in the sequence). Tommy ends his story; Renton's voice-over takes us back to the freeze-frame of Begbie; the image moves, and the main storyline recommences as the glass pursues its vicious trajectory. So the sequence embeds a flashback (the pool game) within a flashforward (Tommy's flat); intertwines three stories (Begbie causing trouble in the pub/the switching of tapes in Tommy's flat/the pool game); and moves the immediate locus of narration from Begbie to Renton (as narrator) to Tommy to Renton (as character) to Tommy to Renton (as narrator) and back to Begbie! Crucially, however, this intricacy never issues in obscurity or opacity – those hallmarks of classical European art cinema. The overriding impression is, rather, one of economy and wit.

These strategies are taken a step further in those sequences which not only crosscut or embed distinct spaces, but fuse real with hallucinated space. In the 'Perfect Day' sequence, point-of-view shots bordered on each side by red carpet render Renton's sinking sensation as he removes himself from the world on a heroin high. In the next scene, during his enforced withdrawal from heroin, Renton is haunted by a baby which crawls along the ceiling, its head turning through 180 degrees. Later, the sound of a TV rises in the mix: Renton fantasises that his mother and father appear on a quiz show hosted by Dale Winton, in which the smiling compere (and gay icon) asks questions on AIDS, never breaking the anodyne façade of televisual contentment. When Tommy appears in Renton's bedroom, sliding along the wall, he participates in the show, answering a question about the receptors exploited by the HIV virus –

foreshadowing the fact that Tommy himself has contracted the virus. So while the TV show itself is the product of Renton's feverish imagination, for a period the game show takes on a kind of diegetic solidity, interacting with the fantastic figures peopling his bedroom. And characteristically, this blurring of subjective and objective space is conjoined with a darkly humorous treatment of AIDS.

Begbie holds court in the pub

Freeze-frame – Renton's voice-over takes over

Flashforward to Tommy's flat

Renton switches the tapes

Flashback to Begbie ripping the pool table

The plasticity and mobility of Renton's voice-over is a vital part of the film's distinctive flavour. Its lithe omnipresence is most evident in those scenes where there is a kind of 'cross-diegetic' interplay of dialogue. In the opening montage, for example, Renton's complaint that he had to 'endure all manner of cunts' telling him that he shouldn't take heroin is exemplified directly by Bebgie, Tommy and his father in live-action vignettes: characters in the space of the story thus appear to converse with the narrator telling the story, as in Welles's *The Magnificent Ambersons* (1942). While Renton's voice-over dominates the film, there is one moment where the voice of another character – Diane – briefly assumes pre-eminence on the soundtrack, and here too figures inhabiting different spaces are put into an imaginary dialogue. Relocated in London, Renton reads a letter sent by Diane, vocalised by Diane on the soundtrack, the letter ending with the news about Begbie's robbery. Renton's doorbell rings; he pauses, and Diane's voice repeats the words 'Francis Begbie'. Just as Renton-the-narrator acts as an omnipresent master of ceremonies through much of the film, here it is as if Diane-as-narrator announces and brings Begbie back into Renton's life (ironically, since as we noted earlier, Diane-as-character is the catalyst for Renton's move to London).

So, many of the sounds in the film enjoy a kind of freedom of movement across time and space. Music often plays a vital role in this respect: in compressing time, and thus accelerating the speed of the story; in enabling the traversal of spatial and diegetic boundaries; and, very importantly, in giving expression to the possibility of transcendence (though, as we will see, music also functions to express more negative emotions). Thus, 'Atomic' compresses several hours of action and fuses disparate locations, and the song shifts from serving a diegetic role (the music playing in the club) to a non-diegetic one (the song rises in volume and envelops the sexual action in the three bedrooms). Renton's leap from the wall to the interior of Swanney's flat is timed to coincide with the end of Blur's 'Sing', the attack of the last chord synchronised precisely with Renton's landing. The elegance of the moment arises from its exacting choreography; its physical grace evokes a kind of spiritual grace, the transcendence of material circumstances through aesthetic – this time musical – redemption. More sustained examples of the role of music in the film's supple narration include the reprise of the opening chase, and the 'cold turkey' sequence, in which Renton is forced off heroin by his parents.

The chase is repeated following the scene in which Allison's baby, Dawn, is discovered dead in her cot – dead from the neglect and selfishness which rule among the junkies. As this scene ends, a distraught Allison cries while Renton rushes to prepare a fix. His voice-over reflects on the fact that 'it wasn't just the baby that died that day – something inside Sick Boy was lost and never returned', and 'Sing' begins faintly. Then the film cuts to the chase. Though there are additional and variant shots here, it is recognisably the same chase that we see at the beginning of the film. But a fundamentally different tone now informs the action, effected not only by the new context (the chase now follows the death of a baby), but by a very different piece of music and voice-over narration. In place of Renton's droll 'choose life' oration, his voice-over now speaks bitterly of the desperate cycle of depression, pain and addiction to which heroin has led the junkies. In place of the stomp and strut of 'Lust for

Life' is the distant, melancholy air of 'Sing', the song's quietly insistent rhythm and circular melody expressing the sense of an empty, lifeless routine. (There is a melodic break in the song, which lifts Damon Albarn's voice up through the scale in a gesture evocative of hope, but this moment in the song doesn't arrive until the subsequent scene in the court, when Renton is let off with a suspended sentence.) The expression of exhilaration on Renton's face in the opening scene becomes a grimace of pain; the dull greyness of Edinburgh suddenly becomes palpable; the manic laughter directed at the driver who almost runs into Renton becomes hollow; and the scene ends with Renton tackled and caught by the authorities.

Renton grimaces

The later 'cold turkey' sequence is, like the sequences accompanied by 'Atomic' and 'Sing', structured to a large degree around a piece of pre-existing music – this time 'Dark and Long (Dark Train Mix)' by Underworld. The music commences immediately after Renton is bolted into his bedroom by his parents, and runs through to a transitional shot of a motorway and housing estate, initiating the subsequent scene in Tommy's flat. Most of the action in the sequence depicts Renton's delirium as he comes off heroin: apparitions in the form of Diane as a flirtatious schoolgirl, a self-righteous Begbie, Spud in prison garb, Tommy looking wasted from heroin, and the dead baby, reveal his fears and feelings of guilt. Visits by his parents and Sick Boy penetrate, but also become caught up in, his hallucinatory daze; everything is coloured by the pain of withdrawal, every movement and sound a heavy blow on Renton's overdriven nervous system.

If in the case of 'Lust for Life' and 'Sing' we see how a piece of music can radically inflect the emotional quality of a stretch of visually rendered action, in this case we see how the image can 'fix' the mood and meaning of a piece of music. 'Dark and Long' is a dance-oriented piece of music. The piece does not have a particularly strong emotional character, aside from the hedonistic associations brought into play by its compulsive groove. But to the extent that the song has an upbeat character, this is put into reverse by its use here. The song and the sequence maintain the sense of a 'rush', but instead of the sudden, giddy headiness that we usually associate with that word, here the sensation evoked is one of nausea and constant sensory overstimulation. The rhythm of the music imposes a relentless quality, the steadiness of the beat suggestive of the way that Renton cannot get off this ride. (Again the visual imagery here is important in supporting this characterisation of the music: in addition to the train motif on the wallpaper, the walls themselves appear to slide away from Renton at one point early in the sequence, as if he is on a train moving through a tunnel.) The first half of the song is almost wholly rhythmic and percussive, the only fragments of melodic sound – Diane singing New Order's 'Temptation', the mechanical strains of a music box, the gaudy flourish of a quiz show fanfare – clashing discordantly. Throughout, 'Dark and Long' acts as a base for other dissonant sounds, like the cry of the baby and the rattle of Spud's chains, which compound the sonic harshness of the sequence.

As I suggested at the outset, the generally propulsive pacing and malleable time and space of *Trainspotting* stand in contrast to the ordinary scene, or at least, the ordinary scene as it used in this film. We've already seen one important example, when Spud sings 'Two Little Boys' after Tommy's funeral, where the marked decrease in tempo, and the absence of any narrational hijinks, allow for a solemn pause in the development of the narrative. Two other examples stand out, the first prefiguring Spud's rendition of 'Two Little Boys', and the occasion provoking Renton's despairing leap. After Spud and Renton's trial for shoplifting, the group meet in the local pub for a celebratory drink – the same pub that they will meet in to commemorate Tommy. The celebrations are qualified, however, by the fact that Spud has been jailed; and a definite damper is put on matters when Spud's mother arrives. Renton – in another of those

'Two Little Boys'

Stillness and fast motion

Tommy's housing scheme

Tommy

redeeming moments – apologises to her, admitting that it is unfair that he goes free while Spud is imprisoned. Spud's mother maintains a weary, dignified silence, retreating after a few seconds, even as she is vitriolically condemned by Begbie for her son's failings. The scene is edited together on the basis of the simple functionality of continuity principles, with none of the self-conscious, playful virtuosity that dominates the film. If in this sequence it is Spud who haunts the group with his absence, in the later 'Two Little Boys' sequence it will be Tommy; in each case the dramatic directness of the ordinary scene is vital in supporting the emotional weight of the two scenes.

The other key example of the emotionally loaded used of the ordinary scene occurs after the transitional shot of the housing estate at the end of 'Dark and Long', where Renton visits a listless, defeated Tommy. They talk about HIV: 'that's nice,' Tommy says sourly, when Renton tells him that he isn't HIV positive. Tommy asks Renton if he has any heroin on him, and then if he can borrow money from him – to which Renton sadly (he knows exactly what the money will be spent on), and yet happily (he wants to connect with Tommy), agrees. As with the other ordinary scenes under discussion here, the action moves forward slowly and awkwardly, with relatively little dialogue, no accompanying music and a great many pauses and silences. The slow pacing of this scene is made particularly emphatic by the contrast with the preceding sequence. Not only is this sequence set to the fast rhythm of 'Dark and Long', its last two shots incorporate fast-motion: first when we see Renton at the bingo club with his parents, an island of static misery amidst the frenetic, speeded-up bingo players; then immediately following this, traffic flies by in fast-motion on the motorway in front of the housing estate. In both shots, fast-motion is set against stasis, 'overtonally' prefiguring the funereal mood of the sad encounter between Tommy and Renton that ensues. In each of these cases, the ordinary scene is used to articulate a slower narrative movement; to allow a pause for reflection, on the part of characters and audience; and to register and emphasise emotions associated with loss, regret and guilt.

7 Scoring *Trainspotting*

Everyone knows what happened to popular music in the early 1960s: the Beatles happened, and they set a trend. The dominant American traditions were appropriated by British musicians and inflected in distinctive ways, and the balance of creative power shifted. Britain became a small superpower in the world of pop music, a position it has maintained, if not quite at the spectacular level achieved in the mid-1960s. There is nothing to compare with this cultural shift in the world of film-making. While members of the British film establishment have occasionally (and optimistically) aped the rhetoric of the British music industry – think of Colin Welland's Oscar-winning speech declaration, 'the British are coming!', evoking the idea of the 'British invasion' of the US led by the Merseybeat bands – the British film industry as a whole remains a small, marginal affair, economically and culturally.[31] Some part of the success and unusual prominence of *Trainspotting* can be ascribed to the way the film appeared as a *musical* phenomenon, a film that had at least as much to do with Britpop, and various earlier trends in British (and American) music, as it did with any traditions of British film-making. Welsh has remarked that Reed and Pop were more important influences on the novel than any writer, and the film certainly honours this dimension of the novel by placing collaborations between Bowie and Reed and Bowie and Pop at the hub of the film's musical structure. But the film does more than merely reiterate the musical references of the novel. By basing the score around these songs, and making the songs so much more than aural wallpaper, the film makes the music itself palpable. It would be hard to overestimate the 'value added' by the songs to the meaning and emotional force of the film.[32]

The score of the film is almost entirely comprised of pre-recorded music – pop songs, along with two cues (discrete musical segments) drawn from the classical tradition (*Carmen* and a chorale prelude by Bach). This collage of pop songs situates the film squarely within contemporary scoring practice, though the score is perhaps unusually extensive.[33] Such collage scores are often assumed to represent the triumph of commercial over aesthetic logic, resulting in incoherence and the dissipation of narrative unity. Yet there is nothing chaotic or casual about *Trainspotting*'s score. Far from being a random smorgasbord of songs, most of the pieces in *Trainspotting* fall into three clear groupings according to style and era: the David Bowie/Lou Reed/Iggy Pop axis from the 1970s; the Britpop of Pulp, Blur, Elastica and Sleeper of the 1990s; and the 1990s techno-dance music of Bedrock and Ice MC. Interestingly, the two final musical cues in the film, from Leftfield and Underworld, represent a kind of fusion of techno with musical elements derived from rock; in this sense there is a kind of 'narrative' implicit in the ordering of the music itself, quite aside from the dramatic functions it performs. In addition to the core groupings and their representatives listed so far, there are a number of songs by contemporaries and fellow travellers: the piece by Eno thus relates to the Bowie grouping, while the song by Primal Scream is aligned with those of both the Britpoppers and the dance-rock outfits.

There are what appear to be some 'rogue' cues which fall outside of these groupings – not only the two classical cues, but Heaven 17's 'Temptation' and New Order's 'Temptation' (two different songs; the latter appears both in its recorded version and twice as a fragment sung by a character within the film). But in fact these cues form the basis of a further, and crucial, 1980s grouping, established more indirectly and cunningly, but no less palpably. While the Eno, Heaven 17 and New Order cues are the only pieces which were recorded and released in the 1980s, many of the 1990s bands featured – several of which were riding high at the time of *Trainspotting*'s release – hark back in one way or another to the 1980s. Sleeper's contribution, 'Atomic', is a cover of a song by Blondie, a number one hit in 1980; Pulp and Primal Scream had been active recording bands since the 1980s; and Blur and Elastica overtly refer back, stylistically, to punk and new wave acts of the early 1980s (like Wire). So, in addition to the three core musical groupings, the film also establishes a musical timeline running from the early 1970s ('Perfect Day' was released in 1972) through to the time of the film's release (the recordings by Primal Scream, Sleeper, Pulp, Leftfield and Damon Albarn are all dated 1996 on the accompanying CD), even though the timeline is not laid out in a simple chronological fashion. Instead, through an intricate cross-referencing of era, style and influence, the film creates a complex musical weave, varied in style, mood and function.

The significance of the songs in *Trainspotting*, and in particular their place within the film's mobile narration, is evident throughout this study. Here I want to focus on two sequences where the importance and sophistication of the interrelationship between the songs and the action seem inescapable – those employing Lou Reed's 'Perfect Day' and 'Carmen-Habañera', an extract from George Bizet's opera *Carmen*. While certain principles hold for both sequences, they are sufficiently different in character to suggest some of the range and variation in the film's use of music. The two sequences also differ in the extent to which the music dominates the soundtrack, or competes with voice-over and dialogue.

Along with the opening 'Lust for Life' montage, the sequence accompanied by Lou Reed's 'Perfect Day' must rank as among the most celebrated and memorable in the film. This is no doubt due in part to the fact that the song was well-known (originally the B-side of 'Walk on the Wild Side', and a track on the simultaneous album *Transformer*, both hits in the US and Britain) before being used in the film. But the fame of the sequence also arises from the sustained, prominent and complex role that the song plays within it (the song is used in its entirety, and dominates the sound mix throughout, unchallenged by Renton's voice-over).[34] 'Perfect Day' is a kind of epic love song – a sentimental ballad which moves between softly articulated verses and grandly orchestrated choruses. But the song is no ordinary love song – in part, because of the overtones brought to it by its composer and performer.

Reed had been a member of the Velvet Underground, the 1960s group notorious for both musical experimentation and lyrical daring, with songs addressing drug-taking ('Waiting for the Man') and sado-masochism ('Venus in Furs'; the band's name came from a photographic book purporting to depict America's 'sexual corruption'), among other hitherto taboo subjects. The Velvets' song 'Heroin', from 1967's *The Velvet Underground and Nico*, casts heroin as the singer-narrator's lover and spouse: 'Heroin, be the death of me/Heroin, it's my wife and it's my life.' The album from which 'Perfect Day' is drawn, *Transformer*, is a kind of panorama of the New York underground ('Walk on the Wild Side', most famously, is an affectionate ode to Warhol's Factory entourage of queers, hustlers, drag queens and junkies). Produced by David Bowie and Mick

Ronson, whose influence is pervasive on *Transformer*, the 'Unholy Trinity' of Bowie, Reed and Pop became synonymous with drug use (as well as, in the case of Bowie and Reed, androgyny, bisexuality and post-1960s libertinism in general).[35]

Against this backdrop, then, it is not hard to see why 'Perfect Day' is something other than the simple paean to friendship and love that it might appear to be. We might well take 'Perfect Day' for an innocent love song if all we hear is a fragment of its triumphal, soaring chorus, as we might do in an ad or indeed in another film; but what is distinctive here is that the film appropriates the whole song, drawing out and exploiting all of its emotional colours. Among these are some distinctly dark shades intimated by the song, even if the nature of these sinister elements remains ambiguous. For Nick Cave, these darker qualities are the ones that make a love song authentic: 'the love song is never simply happy … It must first embrace the potential for pain … The love song must resonate with the whispers of sorrow and the echoes of grief.'[36] By juxtaposing the song with Renton's trip, *Trainspotting* draws these elements to the surface, interpreting the song, in effect, as a 'drug song'. In doing so, the film builds on the personification of heroin as a charismatic lover established earlier, implicitly by the 'Carmen-Habañera' sequence (I'll return to this point), and explicitly by Sick Boy, who asserts: 'personality – I mean that's what counts, right, personality – that's what keeps a relationship going through the years – like heroin. I mean – heroin's got great fuckin' personality.'

I want to focus on a particular moment in the 'Perfect Day' sequence which lies at the heart of the multilayered narration achieved through the interaction of the song and the narrative action (as it is rendered visually and through dialogue). The moment occurs as the song's (apparently) exultant first chorus begins and we see an ambulance moving left to right in the background (as it has done in an earlier shot), across the end of a street. We need to take note of several things here. First, what is it that gives the song its 'epic' quality as it moves into the chorus? The tentative quality of the opening verse is now overcome by the shift from minor to major key, the emphatic piano chords which shape the chorus, the firmer presence of drum and bass, the reverberant multitracking of Reed's voice, the assertion of the string orchestration (present but barely perceptible during the first verse), and of course, the marked rise in volume in the song as a whole which follows from these shifts. However, this entire movement towards musical grandeur is set in counterpoint to what is occurring visually. The shot of the ambulance cranes down to reveal Renton in the foreground, lying prone in the middle of the road; a solid blanket of dark grey cloud hangs over the otherwise deserted estate; this is the desolate scene that we see as we hear Reed declare 'it's such a perfect day'.

Now at this point we also realise that the ambulance is probably not meant for Renton, since we see the vehicle drive past the street on which Renton lies; in the midst of one of the bleakest moments in the story, the film has playfully misdirected us. Earlier in the sequence, when Swanney offers to call a 'taxi' for Renton, we are led to believe that he means an ambulance, because his question is immediately followed by the sound and the first shot of the ambulance. Now we discover that he really did mean a taxi, emphasising that for Swanney and even Renton, this is an unremarkable event; Renton may be having a bad, potentially fatal reaction to the heroin, but it's nothing to break into a sweat about. This brings to mind a scene cut from the released version of the film, in which

Teatime Summer 1972: David Bowie, Iggy Pop and Lou Reed, Dorchester Hotel (copyright © Mick Rock, 1972, 2001)

'just a perfect day...'

Swanney is recovering in hospital from a leg amputation, the result of a gangrenous infection caused by 'jagging' directly into an artery. Even in this circumstance, Swanney remains incorrigibly cheerful; of all the characters in the film, he above all has genuinely chosen to renounce life, and live with the imminent possibility of injury or death.

As we have seen, the types of music drawn on by *Trainspotting* are diverse, from contemporary electro-pop to a Tin Pan Alley ballad, from proto-punk anthems to classical compositions. This brings to our attention the way in which the film creates a kind of dialogue among its musical fragments. The force and meaning of the score emerges not just from individual musical cues, but from the *contrasts* between pieces of music. The ambiguous, modulated lyricism of 'Perfect Day' is followed by the fast, unrelenting pulse of 'Dark and Long'; the mordant wit of 'Mile End' is succeeded by the hedonistic 'For What You Dream Of'; the spiky, intricate guitar work of '2:1' precedes the lugubrious Bach organ composition, which itself is followed by Spud's plain but heartfelt rendition of 'Two Little Boys'. Perhaps the most dramatic example of this kind of dialectical contrast between successive musical cues occurs at the very beginning of the film, where 'Lust for Life' is succeeded by 'Carmen-Habañera'. Bizet's composition contrasts with Pop's song on almost every level. While 'Lust for Life' is a casually buffed-up piece of garage rock, 'Carmen-Habañera' is an elegant adaptation of a traditional dance form.

The two pieces are separated briefly by the title credit, Bizet's composition beginning over the tail end of this shot and the sound of a train. The incongruity of the music is immediately felt as the film cuts to an establishing shot of Renton's drab, sparely furnished room (see p. 34). As with the songs discussed so far, however, the relationship between the music and the action here is subtle and variable, not simply one of incongruity or ironic contrast. The music is composed of two string voices, in the bass and treble registers. The bass voice repeats a four-note motif, while the dominant treble voice articulates a developing melody; the rhythmic and melodic counterpoint (in the musical sense) between the two voices is suggestive of ritual, choreographed movement, representing the movements of the two lovers in the original opera. Here, however, the dance is between Renton and heroin; and if the composition in its original context is a song of seduction, the action here concerns resisting the seductive pull of – indeed, the addictive craving for – heroin.

For all the passion in Bizet's composition, then, there is a powerful sense of decorum attached to it, at variance with Renton's surroundings and his voice-over, as he nails planks of wood over the door to imprison himself, and lays out the array of items necessary for coming off heroin, including pornography and three buckets (for urine, faeces and vomitus). Yet the decorum of the song is not totally at odds with the action: Renton's approach is systematic and methodical; the very choice of words in the voice-over signals this concern ('urine' rather than 'piss', 'faeces' rather than 'shite', and 'vomitus' rather than 'puke'). And just as Renton's objects accumulate, so the orchestration of the composition builds, with the addition of flute, piano, and trumpet, different instruments assuming the role of lead voice from phrase to phrase.

Everything in place, Renton looks in the mirror: 'All I need is one final hit to soothe the pain while the valium takes effect.' This line of the voice-over coincides with a loud four-note phrase, on the last note of which the film cuts to the planks of wood – now lying on the floor. As the shot tilts up we realise that Renton is on the phone, desperately trying to locate a score. Here the temporal ellipsis so often created through the use of music is enlisted in the service of a kind of comic backflip in the story – a single, exquisitely timed cut encapsulating the collapse of all Renton's careful preparations. Another elliptical joke immediately follows, as the film cuts directly from Renton on the phone ('can you help me out?') to a close-up of the anal opium suppositories he is offered in place of the heroin he was expecting ('what the fuck are these?'). Recall that the film wittily misleads us in a similar fashion in the 'Perfect Day' sequence, drawing us into the mistaken assumption that the ambulance is destined for Renton. If the 'plank' example is like a backflip, the 'ambulance' and 'suppository' examples have the quality of a magician's trick: 'now you see it, now you don't.' Once again the playful, impish spirit of the film is manifest.

Of course, the soundtrack is comprised of much more than the songs, and it is important to understand how the songs are combined with voice-over, dialogue and sound effects in the sound mix. Two sonic motifs stand out in *Trainspotting*'s soundscape. The first is a rushing, 'wind' noise, an expressionistic effect which provides dramatic emphasis, and often signals departures from realism (the sound accompanies, for example, Begbie's arm as it moves backwards to throw the beer glass; Renton as he leaps from the wall; and Renton again as he lurches upright, chemically sprung from his heroin stupor). The second motif involves the juxtaposition of music with, or its abrupt termination by, coarse everyday sounds. We've already seen how 'Dark and Long' acts as a rhythmic bed for various dissonant sounds. Similarly, the majesty of 'Perfect Day' is broken by the sound of a siren and an alarm bell, and the lulling rhythm and muted timbre of 'Deep Blue Day' is curtailed by a door slamming shut and the sound of Renton's squelching, toilet-soaked sneakers. On the morning-after-the-night-before, the quiet ambience of domestic life in Diane's parents' spacious apartment (including Diane singing New Order's 'Temptation' in the shower) is contrasted with Spud's awakening to the sound of a noisy aircraft flying over the housing scheme (sonic pollution to match the tactile and olfactory pollution of his own making that he is about to discover). Allison's screams continue as 'Sing' gradually rises in the sound mix; the sound of Renton's doorbell ringing terminates the

'All I need is one final hit'

A change of heart

'Can you help me out?'

'What the fuck are these?'

kinetic 'Think About the Way', bringing the 'swinging' Renton back down to earth with a bump. And appropriately enough, it is the vicious sound of Begbie smashing a beer glass that truncates 'Statuesque', the song which accompanies the gang's celebrations after the successful drug deal, a song expressive of the buoyant (if jokingly paranoid) mood of the gang. This pattern brings out once again the transcendent power often ascribed to music in the film – its power to lift characters out of confinement to a particular time and place, its ability to transform the most dismal of circumstances. But here, too, the limitation on that power is made apparent by the dead weight of material actuality.

Renton and Spud pay their respects to the old folk

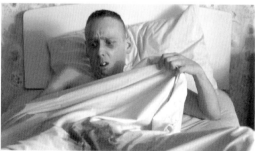

Spud's soiled sheets

8 Black Magic Realism

British cinema is most often associated with a robust social realism, sometimes dour, sometimes mordant – consider the importance, in the canon of British cinema, of the Griersonian documentary tradition, of the Angry Young Man and Free Cinema movements, of Ken Loach, Mike Leigh and Bill Douglas. A straightforward adaptation of Welsh's novel might have fed straight into this tradition, with its stress on working-class culture and vernacular idioms. A large part of the achievement of the film, however, involves a transformation of this realism, accomplished by intensifying the novel's black humour, buoying it up with an effervescent style, fuel-injecting it with the rhythms of pop, and leavening it with fantasy in the manner of magic realism. Elements of magic realism are present in the novel, but the relative weighting of vernacular realism and fantastic transformation in the novel is reversed in the film, the magical elements taking on a much more prominent role in the latter. And here we should note the alternative, non-naturalistic tendencies in the work of Lindsay Anderson, Bill Forsyth, Michael Powell and Emeric Pressburger – an acknowledged influence on Boyle, Hodge and Macdonald's subsequent film, *A Life Less Ordinary* – and the Scottish novelist Alasdair Gray that (directly or indirectly) might have influenced the makers of *Trainspotting*.

Integral to this black magic realism is a concentration on the most dismal aspects of realist *mise en scène*, in order both to draw a kind of gallows humour from them, and to lay the groundwork for a miraculous transformation of them. In this way, black magic realism is closely related to the 'aesthetic redemption' discussed in Chapter 3, 'The City's Ripped Backsides'. One of the few precedents in British cinema for this aesthetic strategy is *My Beautiful Laundrette* (Stephen Frears, 1985). In the midst of a crappy row of shops in a south London neighbourhood, the two central characters (one Pakistani, one white) turn a malfunctioning launderette into a whimsical space with the air of a seaside pier or fairground (a large awning-sign, framed by a semicircle of lights, declares the name 'POWDERS') – in spite of the fact that the launderette remains under siege from racism and other 'realist' forces. *Laundrette* lacks, however, *Trainspotting*'s lively pop-inflected narration, and perhaps for this reason, the magical space of the launderette seems more susceptible to the crippling weight of the generally realist world of the film.

The black humour of *Trainspotting* is intimately related to elements of farce, grotesquerie and comic absurdity. On one end of this scale, there are moments like the theft of the TV from the old people's home – Renton and Spud casually walk into a TV room and calmly remove it while the old folk look on bemused but unprotesting. An alert viewer might be reminded of what the scabrous opening monologue has to say about this sort of scenario,[37] but the humour of the scene itself is gently absurd. At the other end of the scale, the film engages in a dark, often scatological humour which has drawn accusations of 'bad taste' – think here not just of the bookie's toilet, but of Spud's soiled sheets and the baby that menaces Renton as he withdraws from heroin. These scenes, of course, tap into a deep vein of grotesque humour in British culture, from Joe Orton to *Monty Python* (1969–74) and *The Young Ones* (1982–4), Donald McGill's seaside postcards to *Viz*, *Spitting Image* (1984–96) to *Brass Eye* (1997–)

Relief

Paradise lost

Desperation

The lagoon

Paradise regained

and *Jam* (2000–). Setting *Trainspotting* alongside these names and shows, however, reveals the 'bad taste' of the film to be relatively mild. Compare the 'AIDS quiz show' in *Trainspotting* with the jaw-dropping, calculatedly offensive conceits of Chris Morris's *Jam*. In one sketch, a couple talk, with glowing pride, about anally raping their child. Both the *Trainspotting* and the *Jam* scenes take satirical aim at the flattening effect of television, but in using child abuse as the vehicle of satire, the *Jam* sketch breaks one of the strongest taboos of our time – as witness the furore that broke out over the 'paedophilia exposé' episode of Morris's current affairs parody *Brass Eye*. Or compare *Trainspotting*'s 'offences' with the shibboleths around disablement violated by Lars Von Trier's *The Idiots* (1998), about a bunch of middle-class drop-outs who 'spazz out' – pretend to be mentally retarded – as a protest against bourgeois conformity.

The constraint of *Trainspotting* comes into clear focus when set alongside *The Acid House* (a film scripted by Irvine Welsh on the basis of his own short stories). *The Acid House* invests its humour with a confrontational rawness largely absent from *Trainspotting*: in 'The Granton Star Cause', the first of the film's three stories, the protagonist is turned into a fly, feeds on dog shit, witnesses his erstwhile girlfriend in the throes of feral, drug-laced sex with a former five-a-side team-mate, and to cap it off returns home to see his parents engaging in a sado-masochistic sexual ritual – his mother verbally abusing his father while fucking him with a dildo. Much of 'The Acid House', the third of the stories, proceeds through a montage of screaming, psychotic discordance. While *The Acid House* revels in this abrasive comedy of unremitting interpersonal brutality, *Trainspotting* contains its black humour for the sake of a broader range of emotional tones.

Nowhere is the black magic realism of the film better exemplified than in the toilet scene; 'unbearably realistic'[38] in the novel, the film plays off this most sordid of settings against a delirious, comic fantasy space. In its very literalness, the scene seems designed to provoke charges of indulgence in lowly 'toilet humour', while at the same time trumping such charges with its undeniable ingenuity. After relieving himself, Renton realises that in doing so he has expelled the two anal heroin suppositories which he had only just inserted, and starts to fish around in the overflowing, disgusting toilet bowl. Only the scene in which Spud, awakening from a night of incontinent inebriation, splatters his girlfriend's family with his shit-stained sheet as they eat their traditional breakfast tops the coprophilia of Renton's moment of intimacy with the toilet.

So much for the harsh realism and black humour. The moment of magic redemptiveness then follows: as Renton is forced to delve more and more deeply into the bowl, 'Carmen-Habañera' returns to accompany his heedless search, the concluding two-note flourish of the piece coinciding with the sight of Renton disappearing wholesale down the toilet. Emerging on the other side in the sun-dappled tropical pool, echoing to the 'Hawaiian' sound of Eno's 'Deep Blue Day' (as well as a submarine radar sound effect), Renton discovers his suppositories like pearls on a rocky seabed. When Renton surfaces, the suppositories glow luminously, and even when he returns to his flat in the next scene, he is still glistening wet. The boundary between reality and magic is thus permeable, a matter of degree rather than an absolute contrast. By moving seamlessly between the grim detail of ordinary life and a flight of fancy, the scene operates 'magically' not only in formal terms, but thematically too, reiterating the power of heroin to transform – temporarily – the most impoverished real existence into one of sensual richness.

Dark humour, playful narration and stylisation come together again in the film's complex treatment of time. At one extreme, Spud careers through his amphetamine-driven interview, his overheated mind given expression by speed-riffs on the tourist industry and jumpcuts which bounce the viewer around the room, from profile to frontal shots, long shots to close-ups. And in spite of the film's thematic focus on the languorous phenomenology of heroin, the centrality of crosscutting in the film maintains the ecstatic momentum established by the film's explosive opening. At the other extreme, in contrast with the predominantly fast pace of the film, a series of freeze-frames dramatically retard or halt the flow of action. Through these still images, *Trainspotting* dwells on the nature of memory, self-hood and the bonds of friendship. The film establishes a dialectic between restless forward movement, and a series of frozen, Proustian moments which call up and demand reflection on the past.

The freeze-frame is first used in the opening sequence, as a means of introducing the central characters (whose frozen images are labelled with name-titles): Renton is caught with that wild expression on his face as he leans on the bonnet of the car which almost hits him; Sick Boy is frozen in a gesture of pleading self-defence in the five-a-side football game. In the pub sequence, the series of embedded narrations is initiated by a freeze-frame on Begbie (see p. 58), and this example reveals some other roles

Spud's interview

played by freeze-framing. Stilling the action on the moment that Begbie casually tosses the glass over his shoulder creates suspense: what on earth is Begbie up to? where is that glass going to land? what will be the aftermath? All of these questions remain suspended while the film takes us forward to Tommy's room, and back to the pool game, until we return to the frozen image of Begbie and the action moves on.

Introductory freeze-frame

In creating suspense, the freeze-frame points us forward in time (what is *going* to happen?); but the freeze-frame generates another kind of emotion by directing our attention backwards in time. How does it achieve this? Film theorists have argued that the moving, filmic image creates a very different sense of time to that created by the still, photographic image (it is worth noting here that some of the freeze-frames in the film, such as the portrait shots of the five-a-side teams, are presented as still photos). A photograph evokes the sense of what once existed, of the past, of 'having been there-ness'; a film, it is said, fabricates an impression of continuous 'present-ness'. Whatever the truth of these generalisations, the situation is complicated in *Trainspotting* by the voice-over, which alternates between past and present tenses. The present tense is generally reserved for descriptions of 'generic' aspects of junkie life: 'choose life', 'relinquishing heroin', and so forth. The past tense is used, by contrast, to describe the events peculiar to Renton's passage, setting up a temporal disjuncture between the moment of voice-over utterance (the 'present') and the moment of the depicted action (the 'past', relative to the voice-over, but a past which is rendered present to us, by virtue of the power of the moving image). This disjuncture is only closed in the film's final moments as the voice-over seems to assume the role of 'speaking' Renton's thoughts as he crosses the Thames.

By drawing on the powerful association of the still photograph with that-which-is-past, however, the freeze-frames establish a third layer of temporality, still more remote from the 'present' of the voice-over:

voice-over	moving image	freeze-frames
present	'present-past'	past

Thus, when the shot of Begbie is frozen, it is as if we are looking at an image from a photographic album, of a past moment. This is underlined by Renton's voice-over, which is literally in the past tense, and acts as a vehicle for Renton's reflection on what he was and what he has become (think of Begbie as Renton's tea-dipped madeleine). Recall, also, that we return to this still image after the digression concerning the pool game. By recapitulating this moment in the story, and showing it in a different light on each occasion, the freeze-frame on Begbie in the pub performs in miniature the task undertaken by the reprise of the opening sequence on a larger scale. In each case, a kind of narrative loop is created which, by virtue of its repetition of a moment in the story and the combination of this moment with voice-over narration in the past tense, casts that stretch of action into the past of the story in a way that cannot be achieved with more straightforward, linear storytelling.

The freeze-frames thus not only remind us that Renton is the film's *meneur de jeu*, that this is above all his story, but also bestow upon the story a touch of nostalgia, in spite of the cynical tone of the voice-over. To be sure, by the end of the film, when we reach the 'present' moment of the voice-over, Renton is relieved to be leaving his past behind; but this does not entirely erase the memories of the good times, and the metamorphosis of the not-so-good into the good by the deceptive slights of memory. The freeze-frames dispersed across the film play their part in creating the elegaic countercurrent which runs against the tide of Renton's jaundiced view of the past.

The end credit sequence also uses a series of still frames of the major characters, perhaps functioning to create a kind of nostalgia *for the film*. That is, if the stills in the body of the film generate the sense of a time past for the characters in the story, then these stills begin to memorialise the film itself, by offering us a series of 'snapshots' of the major characters (and of the performers, for the stills here represent the performers playing the roles as much as – if not more than – the characters themselves). And in doing this, they exploit that same process of transmutation at work implicitly in the film's earlier use of freeze-frames: catching a character in

an instant of time, they are abstracted from the complexity of what lies behind and ahead of this moment, from his or her interrelations with other characters – in short, from the fullness that we derive from a narrative proper. The stills here do not erase this complexity, nor our memory of the uglier qualities of the characters and moments of despair in the narrative, but they do move such things out of the foreground as the film concludes (and so make emotional space for the redemption discussed earlier). The freeze-frame motif thus balances several contrasting emotions on a knife-edge, pitting the comedy of Begbie's blustering arrogance against his truly appalling violence as well as, in spite of it all, a trace of regretful sadness. After all, he's a mate, so what can you do?

9 Moving On

SICK BOY: … at one point you've got It, then you lose It, and It's gone forever. All walks of life. Georgie Best, for example, had It, lost It. Or David Bowie, or Lou Reed … Charlie Nicholas, David Niven, Malcolm McClaren, Elvis Presley …

RENTON: So, we all get old, we cannae hack it any more, and that's it?

Why is it worth pouring out all these words on *Trainspotting* – a film that many would regard as at best an effective, if ephemeral, piece of popular entertainment, and at worst a pernicious slice of drug mythology? *Trainspotting* justifies and rewards sustained consideration not only in terms of its cultural impact in general and its significance for Scottish and British film culture in particular, but above all for its accomplishment as a work of art. *Trainspotting* really is a 'modern classic'.

Signs of the cultural impact of *Trainspotting* – novel and film – are everywhere. Switch on the TV and listen to the number of shows which use songs from the soundtrack – most spectacularly, 'Perfect Day' reappearing as the basis of a BBC promotional film in 1998. Consider the various iconic moments, characters and images from the film which have become dependably understood reference points: Renton and Spud racing headlong towards the camera; a bedraggled Renton emerging from the toilet; Begbie as the embodiment of violent masculinity. Contemplate the influence of the film on the image of Scotland and Britain internationally, roughening up and troubling the familiar imagery of Britain's aristocratic legacy, its imperial grandeur, its honourable working-class folk – the Britain of heritage, literary adaptation, romantic comedy, home improvement and gardening. Look at the string of films which have tried to mimic aspects of *Trainspotting* (its dramatic world, its style, tone and iconography), including *Twin Town* (Kevin Allen, 1997), *The Life of Stuff* (Simon Donald, 1997), *Looking After Jo Jo* (John MacKenzie, 1998), *Lock, Stock and Two Smoking Barrels* (1998), *Human Traffic* (Justin Kerrigan, 1999), *Beautiful Creatures* (Bill Eagles, 2000), *Sorted* (Alexander Jory, 2000) and *Late Night Shopping* (Saul Metzstein, 2001). Many such films have missed the mark, much in the way that Quentin Tarantino's success led to a slew of half-baked attempts to emulate

Familiar heritage
iconography

Garbage imagery

'Freaky' imagery

the style of *Reservoir Dogs* and *Pulp Fiction*. Like any fresh style, the
imagery of *Trainspotting* is itself susceptible to congealing into a new set of
clichés.

But all of this begs a deeper and more difficult question: what makes
Trainspotting a very good, perhaps even a great, film? As I hope my
discussion of the film has demonstrated, *Trainspotting* is a dense, finely

crafted, sophisticated film, inventive in its approach to its subject matter, encompassing tones from the exuberant to the elegaic. A film of great stylistic panache, it is nevertheless far from glib. *Trainspotting* is both emotionally and intellectually complex, often bringing together contrasting emotions in a single scene or moment, and shot through with what I have termed an 'aesthetically redemptive' attitude, which offers a more subtle vision of the world than either straight-ahead realism or escapism. The film is honest and unflinching in its depiction of heroin addiction, but neither maudlin nor ploddingly worthy nor smugly miserabilist (self-satisfied with the bleakness of the world it depicts). It provides an articulate, authentic voice for a world not often represented, and a voice that speaks to a large audience, in spite of its idiosyncracies.

For some critics, it is precisely the authenticity of the film's treatment of heroin use that is in doubt, the 'freaky imagery', 'nifty soundtrack' and charismatic, physically attractive hero betraying the miserable truth about heroin addiction.[39] The film 'can't let boredom be boring', is 'unable to call a turd a turd'[40] and ultimately buys into Welsh's vision of the junkie as a 'closet romantic', a figure of heroic, highly individualistic, resistance, rather than one of tragic self-destruction in a desperate social climate. Although liberating himself, Renton remains psychologically trapped within the selfish, individualistic culture of his times, unconcerned with the punters who will now be ripped off by the gear he's sold, blind to the more communal values of the rave culture he briefly encounters, seeing in it only more egoism ('just wankers'). Individual liberation obscures any vision of social emancipation.

These worries amount to a kind of interdiction on aesthetic licence, implying that only the most literal-minded, leaden-footed realism is (morally) appropriate for a subject as serious as heroin. I have argued, on the contrary, that the related strategies of aesthetic redemption and black magic realism depict both the reality of heroin use (its causes and possible effects, good and ill) while also representing the spirit of resistance (Welsh's 'romanticism'), and desire for transformation, which motivates its use in the first place. Something more than realism is necessary to capture this complex of states. Certainly the film is (mildly) 'delinquent' – Raul Ruiz's term for art which prioritises the expression of transgressive ideas and sensibilities over a sense of social responsibility. But while the ending of the film is anything but downbeat, no one who reflects on the implications of the movie as a whole will come away with the idea that heroin is just a blast.

Trainspotting struck a chord with a large audience because it addresses big issues with a deceptively light touch, drawing on and synthesising all manner of cultural and artistic traditions – regional, national and international. In discussing these concerns at the outset, the issue at stake was the cultural identity of the film: the extent to which it can be called a Scottish or a British film, the kind of audiences it seems to address, the folding in of American ingredients within its Scottish base. This is a process that involves not only the 'Americanisation' of Scottish and British culture, but the transformation of American culture as it interacts with these cultures, *and* the selling of these cultures back to American and other international audiences. Behind these very modern concerns, however, lies something more traditional, for it is (among other things) this very compound of elements that makes the film so aesthetically compelling.

The novelist Jonathan Coe has related how, staying in a tiny village in the La Mancha region of Spain, the only 'English'-language novel available was *Trainspotting*. For Coe, the anecdote provides evidence that good regional fiction has an international audience. But we can go further. The international success of *Trainspotting* suggests how the film at once captures and condenses the currents of the time and place of its making, and at the same time transforms these immediate matters into themes, questions and stories with universal resonance, taking on what the philosopher Georg Hegel would call 'world-historical' significance.[41] Poverty, intravenous drug use and the AIDS epidemic struck Edinburgh in a particularly devastating way, but of course the film is not merely about these specific phenomena: it is also, among other things, about misery, joy, comradeship, betrayal and the freedom to move on.

What of the broader impact of the film on the British film industry and British film culture? Hailed at the time of its release as a landmark film, heralding an emerging vitality in British film-making, it would be hard to maintain that those hopes have been realised. Boyle, Hodge and Macdonald have themselves faltered with their subsequent films, achieving nothing with the same range, depth and cohesion as *Trainspotting*. If the film is a landmark, it is one after the fashion of Anthony Gormley's *Angel of the North* sculpture – a striking monument in an otherwise bland landscape. It is certainly true that, in purely quantitative terms, British film-making is in an improved state of health: cinema audiences are larger, more films are funded, and more of these films find distribution, than was the case ten years ago. But since the modest improvements in the infrastructure of production and distribution have not led to a stream of impressive movies – nothing that would lead one to anoint a British 'new wave' – one can only draw the conclusion that the malaise in British film-making resides at a deeper and more elusive level. This relates not only to the way in which indigenous film-making is hobbled by relatively low investment levels and the continuing domination of distribution by American companies, but also to the place of cinema within British culture.

British cinema is caught between the power of Hollywood, the occasional contempt of our French neighbours, and the substantial achievements of both. But it also labours under the weight of a vein of self-loathing and self-flagellation, itself connected with the Amerophilia discussed earlier in this book. For some critics, *Trainspotting* was too 'American' – too stylish, dynamic, upbeat; for others, our cinema is not American enough. (I suspect that, both for those who decry and those who applaud the film, the 'American' overtones of Renton's ultimate triumph have much to do with their reactions.) British cinema is perpetually caught on the horns of this dilemma.

So rather than bemoaning all the bad and (more often) mediocre films which Britain produces, let us end by focusing on the fact that Britain has produced some great films and film-makers, that there really is nothing inherently 'incompatible' about the ideas of 'Britain' and 'cinema'. Not that there is anything to be complacent about in this respect. Perhaps Sick Boy's brutal 'unifying theory of life' carries more than a grain of truth: most of us, in whatever endeavour we choose to pursue – 'all walks of life' – only manage to put it all together, just so, once in a blue moon. We have It, then It deserts us. If Boyle and company never quite find It again, we should nevertheless cherish the fact that they mastered It so fully with *Trainspotting*.

Notes

1 Throughout I will refer to Boyle, Hodge and Macdonald as the principal authors of *Trainspotting*. This in no way is meant to slight the vital contributions of their various creative collaborators, including Kave Quinn's production design, Brian Tufano's cinematography and Masahiro Hirakubo's editing.

2 'We didn't want *Short Cuts*' : Hodge, quoted on the Cannes Film Festival webpage devoted to *Trainspotting*.

3 The rest of this (highly pertinent) sentence reads: '… and therefore the best films ever made: *The Godfather*, *Godfather Part II*, *Taxi Driver*, *Goodfellas* and *Reservoir Dogs*.' Nick Hornby, *High Fidelity* (1995; London: Penguin, 2000), p. 21.

4 Ryan Gilby, 'Under the Influence', *Premiere*, vol. 4 no. 2, March 1996, p. 62.

5 On the influence of art schools on British pop, see Simon Frith and Howard Horne, *Art into Pop* (London: Methuen, 1987).

6 From the *Feed Daily* website editorial, 23 May 1997.

7 Duncan Petrie, *Screening Scotland* (London: BFI, 2000), p. 196.

8 Simon Reynolds, 'High Society', *Artforum*, Summer 1996, p. 15.

9 Boyle's remark is reported in 'Drugs Film Attacked for Glamorising Heroin', *Independent*, 16 February 1996, p. 6.

10 Irvine Welsh, 'City Tripper', *Guardian,* 16 February 1996, section 2, p. 4. Rankin's comments were made in an edition of *The South Bank Show* devoted to his work, June 2001.

11 From 'Sister Ray', on the Velvet Underground's *White Light/White Heat* (1968).

12 The original, literal notion of trainspotting has gradually enlarged, so that 'trainspotter' can be applied metaphorically to any obsessive pursuit (one can be a film or music trainspotter, for example), and numerous variations have been spawned, such as 'planespotter' and (from the world of music fandom) 'samplespotter' and 'breakspotter'.

13 Although obviously very different films in a host of ways, there are some surprising similarities between *Trainspotting* and *Braveheart*. Consider the following passage from Welsh's novel, which might have acted as inspiration for a large part of *Braveheart*'s narrative: 'Scotland the brave, ma arse; Scotland the shitein cunt. We'd throttle the life oot ay each other fir the privilege ay rimmin some English aristocrat's piles. Ah've never felt a fuckin thing aboot countries, other than total disgust.' Irvine Welsh, *Trainspotting* (1993; London: Vintage, 1999), p. 228.

14 Welsh, *Trainspotting*, p. 166.

15 Quoted in Nicholas Wroe, 'The Guardian Profile: James Kelman', *Guardian*, 2 June 2001, *Review*, p. 7.

16 Quoted in 'It's Such a Perfect Day', *Premiere*, vol. 4 no. 2, March 1996, p. 60.

17 On this notion, see Paul Gilroy, *There Ain't No Black in the Union Jack: The Cultural Politics of Race and Nation* (London: Routledge, 1987), pp. 43–71.

18 In fact, the scene was shot at Corrour Station on Rannoch Moor, to the northwest of Glasgow, rather than in the Pentland hills south of Edinburgh, where the action most plausibly takes place. But there is more than simply the 'creative geography' deployed by almost all films at work here, whereby disparate locations are stitched together to create a unified, fictional reality. The strategy here rather resembles the 'creative derangement' of landscape films like John Smith's *The Black Tower* (1987) and Patrick Keillor's *London* (1994), which use framing and editing to create a strange, sometimes shifting, impression of the landscapes they depict.

19 Welsh, 'City Tripper', p. 4.

20 Perhaps the residue of the 'Cock Problems' chapter in the novel: 'It's fuckin grotesque tryin tae find an inlet. Yesterday ah hud tae shoot intae ma cock, where the most prominent vein in ma body is. Ah dinnae want tae get intae that habit' (Welsh, *Trainspotting*, p. 86).

21 'The city's ripped backsides' – from Iggy Pop's 'The Passenger', on *Lust for Life* (1977).

22 For Boyle, Hodge and Macdonald's thoughts on realism, and their attempts to sidestep it in *Trainspotting*, see 'The Boys are Back in Town', interview with Geoffrey Macnab, *Sight and Sound*, vol. 6 no. 2, February 1996, p. 10.

23 In this respect, the film is true in spirit to the letter of the novel: Renton is described there as loving (fraternally, platonically) Spud (Welsh, *Trainspotting*, p. 343).

24 In the promotional material for the film, Diane is in effect made a member of the gang, displacing Tommy, by occupying one of the five portrait slots, alongside Renton, Begbie, Sick Boy and Spud (see p. 6). However, additional scenes involving Diane were cut during editing. Ironically, then, while the actual film narrowed its focus around the male fraternity, the marketing of the film promoted the idea that Diane would have a greater presence in the story than she does – presumably as a way of countering the impression that the film would have a narrow, male appeal.

25 John Hodge, 'Introduction', *Trainspotting and Shallow Grave* (London: Faber and Faber, 1996), p. x.

26 Other signs of the film's efforts to accrue countercultural kudos include Sick Boy's caustic dismissal of the Oscars, and, on the marketing front, the organisation of a midnight screening at the Cannes Film Festival (following in the footsteps of *Reservoir Dogs*, and more generally evoking the outlandish, oppositional reputation of the 'midnight movie' tradition). Rejected by festival boss Gilles Jacob for the official competition, the film's producers turned this to the advantage of the film, circulating the idea that the film was 'too dangerous' for Establishment Cannes.

27 Friedrich Nietzsche, *The Anti-Christ*, section 21, in *Basic Writings*, trans. Walter Kaufman (New York: Random House, 1967).

28 The mocking transvaluation of Christian ideals is made explicit and fused with parodic list-making in Irvine Welsh's *Glue* (London: Jonathan Cape, 2001), in which the Ten Commandments are replaced by an alternative set of Welshworld rules, coalescing around male tribal loyalty.

29 '[In Christianity] body is despised … Christian is all hatred of the senses, of joy in the senses, of joy in general' (Nietzsche, *The Anti-Christ*, section 21).

30 A classic discussion of the scene and other sequence types in film can be found in Christian Metz, 'Problems of Denotation in the Fiction Film', in *Film Language: A Semiotics of the Cinema*, trans. Michael Taylor (Chicago, IL: University of Chicago Press, 1991).

31 While American films dominate the British film market, British pop acts dominate the British music market; British music has a substantially greater presence in America than does British film-making; and while of the six major musical corporations dominating world markets one (EMI) is British-based, none of the major film corporations are British-based or owned. Not coincidentally, the compilation CD based on *Trainspotting* was released by EMI (even though the film was distributed by Dutch rival PolyGram).

32 'Added value' is a concept drawn from the work of French film critic, film-maker and composer Michel Chion. The concept draws attention to the way music (or any kind of sound) may 'add' to or fundamentally affect the meaning or tone of a film sequence, even as we mistakenly ascribe this meaning uniquely to the visual elements in the sequence. See Michel Chion, *Audio-Vision: Sound on Screen*, trans. Claudia Gorbman (New York: Columbia University Press, 1994).

33 While a classical score typically occupied three-quarters of a film's duration, the collage score, as it emerged in the 1960s and 1970s, typically occupied only one quarter of a film's duration. *Trainspotting*'s score is closer to the classical norm, suggesting both the variety of functions it performs within the film, and the significance of the score to the film as a whole. On the history of the pop score, see Jeff Smith, *The Sounds of Commerce: Marketing Popular Film Music* (New York: Columbia University Press, 1998).

34 Will Self's reaction to this scene provides a clear example of the entrenched prejudice that 'music video' and 'art' are mutually exclusive categories: 'I began to feel as if I was watching an extended pop video, rather than a work of filmic art.' Will Self, 'Carry on up the Hypodermic', *Observer*, 11 February 1996, *Preview*, p. 9. My view is that the scene succeeds as art precisely because of its masterly integration of musical and narrative elements.

35 Ironically, Bowie has often been accused of 'sanitizing genuine innovators [like Pop and Reed] for public consumption', in much the same way that the film *Trainspotting* is seen by some to sanitise Welsh's novel. In a double irony, the film incorporates exactly this sentiment in the form of Sick Boy's speech about the inevitable decline of all great artists, in which Bowie and Reed are both cited, even as the film uses music from all three musicians which, on this view, has been 'sanitised'; or, as Sick Boy puts it, is 'just shite' (Lou Reed's solo work is the explicit target of this jibe). Quotation from Clinton Heylin, *From the Velvets to the Voidoids* (London: Penguin, 1993), p. 41.

36 Nick Cave, 'Love is the Drug', *Guardian* 21 April 2001, *Weekend*, p. 53.

37 'Choose rottin' away at the end of it all, pissin' your last in a miserable home, nothin' more than an embarrassment to the selfish, fucked up brats that you've spawned to replace yerselves.'

38 Sarah Street, *British National Cinema* (London: Routledge, 1997), p. 111.

39 Self, 'Carry on up the Hypodermic', p. 8. Self's view of the film as a kind of 'drug pornography' is countered by the reactions of the recovered heroin addicts, from the Calton Athletic Recovery Group, who acted as 'technical advisors' on the film (and appear as the five-a-side team opposing Renton and company in the opening sequence). See Rebecca Fowler, 'Trainspotting: That's Just the Way it is', *Independent*, 10 February 1996, *Weekend*, pp. 7–8.

40 Quotations from Reynolds, 'High Society', p. 16; Gilby, review of *Trainspotting*, *Premiere*, vol. 4 no. 2, March 1996, p. 9.

41 G. W. F. Hegel, *Aesthetics: Lectures on Fine Art Vol. 1*, trans. T. M. Knox (Oxford: Clarendon Press, 1975), pp. 263–80.

Credits

TRAINSPOTTING

United Kingdom
1995

Director
Danny Boyle
Producer
Andrew Macdonald
Screenplay
John Hodge
Based on a novel by Irvine
Welsh
Director of Photography
Brian Tufano
Editor
Masahiro Hirakubo
Production Designer
Kave Quinn
© Channel Four Television
Corporation
Production Companies
Channel Four Films
presents a Figment film in
association with Noel Gay
Motion Picture Company
Ltd for Channel Four
Production Accountant
Jenifer Booth
Production Co-ordinator
Shellie Smith
Production Manager
Lesley Stewart
Location Managers
Robert How
London:
Andrew Bainbridge

London Contact
Lene Bausager
Assistant to the Producer
Jill Robertson
Production Runner
Kristin McDougall
Floor Runners
Aidan Quinn, Michael
Queen
Location Assistants
Saul Metzstein
London:
Charlie Hiscott
1st Assistant Director
David Gilchrist
2nd Assistant Director
Claire Hughes
3rd Assistant Director
Ben Johnson
Casting
Gail Stevens, Andy Pryor
Script Supervisor
Anne Coulter
Focus Puller
Robert Shipsey
Clapper Loader
Lewis Buchan
Camera Trainee
Neil Davidson
Underwater Cameraman
Mike Valentine
**Underwater Camera
Assistant**
Jim Kerr
Steadicam Operator
Simon Bray
Stills Photography
Liam Longman

Grip
Adrian McCarthy
Gaffer
Willie Cadden
Best Boy
Mark Ritchie
Electricians
Arthur Donnelly, Jimmy
Dorigan
Genny Operator
John Duncan
Special Visual Effects
Grant Mason, Tony Steers
Fido Services
Cinesite
Assembly Editor
Anuree De Silva
Assistant Editors
Neil Williams, Denton Brown
FT2 Editing Trainee
Rab Wilson
Editing Facilities
Salon
Art Director
Tracey Gallacher
Assistant Art Director
Niki Longmuir
**Art Department
Assistants**
Irene Harris,
Lorna J. Stewart
Art Department Runners
Miguel Rosenberg-
Sapochnik, Alan Payne
Art Department Trainee
Stephen Wong

Set Dresser
Penny Crawford
Scenic Artist
Stuart Clarke
Draughtspersons
Jean Kerr, Frances Connell
Prop Master
Gordon Fitzgerald
Dressing Props
Piero Jamieson, Mat Bergel
Stand-by Props
Stewart Cunningham,
Scott Keery
Props Driver
Gregor Telfer
Props Trainees
Paul McNamara,
Michelle Bowker
Construction Manager
Colin H. Fraser
**Construction
Chargehand**
Derek Fraser
Stand-by Carpenter
Bert Ross
Stand-by Stagehand
Brian Boyne
Carpenters
Brian Adams, Richard
Hassall, Peter Knotts,
John Watt
Painters
James Patrick, Paul Curren,
Bobby Gee
Stagehand
John Donnelly
Plasterer
Paterson Lindsay

Costume Designer
Rachael Fleming
Wardrobe Supervisor
Stephen Noble
Make-up Design
Graham Johnston
Make-up/Hair
Robert McCann
Titles/Typography
Tomato
Titles/Opticals
Cine Image
Soundtrack
'Lust for Life' by Iggy Pop,
David Bowie, performed by
Iggy Pop; 'Carmen-
Habañera' by Georges
Bizet; 'Deep Blue Day' by
Brian Eno, Daniel Lanois,
Roger Eno, performed by
Brian Eno; 'Trainspotting' by
Bobby Gillespie, Andrew
Innes, Robert Young, Martin
Duffy, performed by Primal
Scream; 'Temptation' by Ian
Marsh, Martyn Ware, Glenn
Gregory, performed by
Heaven 17; 'Atomic' by
Deborah Harry, Jimmy
Destri, performed by
Sleeper; 'Temptation' by
Stephen Morris, Peter Hook,
Bernard Sumner, Gillian
Gilbert, performed by New
Order; 'Nightclubbing' by
Iggy Pop, David Bowie,
performed by Iggy Pop;
'Sing' by Damon Albarn,

Graham Coxon, Alex
James, David Rowntree,
performed by Blur; 'Perfect
Day' by/performed by Lou
Reed; 'Dark and Long
(Dark Train Mix)' by Rick
Smith, Karl Hyde, Darren
Emerson, performed by
Underworld; 'Think about
the Way (Bom Digi Digi
Bom …)' by Roberto
Zanetti, performed by Ice
MC; 'Mile End' by Banks,
Cocker, Doyle, Mackey,
Senior, Webber, performed
by Pulp; 'For What You
Dream Of (Full on
Renaissance Mix)' by John
Digweed, Nick Muir, Carol
Leeming, performed by
Bedrock featuring Kyo; '2:1'
by Donna Lorraine
Matthews, performed by
Elastica; 'Herzlich tut mich
verlangen' by J. S. Bach,
performed by Gabor
Lehotka; 'Two Little Boys' by
Edward Madden, Theodore
Morse, performed by Ewen
Bremner; 'A Final Hit' by
Barnes, Daley, performed
by Leftfield; 'Statuesque' by
Werner, Stewart, Maclure,
Osman, performed by
Sleeper; 'Born Slippy
(Nuxx)' by Rick Smith, Karl
Hyde, performed by
Underworld; 'Closet

Romantic' by Damon Albarn, performed by Albarn, Gauld, Sidwell, Henry, Smith and The Duke Strings Quartet

Sound Recordist
Colin Nicolson

Boom Operator
Tony Cook

Sound Maintenance Engineer
Noel Thompson

Re-recording Mixers
Brian Saunders, Ray Merrin, Mark Taylor

Post-production Sound
The Sound Design Co

Sound Re-recorded at
Delta Sound Services

Dialogue Editor
Richard Fettes

Effects Editor
Jonathan Miller

Footsteps Editor
Martin Cantwell

Special Technical Adviser
Eamon Doherty

Action Vehicles
Robbie Ryan

Tracking Vehicles
Bickers of Coddenham Ltd

Facility Vehicles/Drivers
Bristol Television Film Services Ltd

Camera Car Driver
Eric Smith

Caterers
Guy Cowan, Fiona Cowan, Allan Bell, Jackie Douglas, Isabel Graham, Andy Irvine, John McVeigh, Reel Food

Security
Dennis McFadden, William Adams, James Dunsmuir, William Mackinnon, Ian Miller

Completion Bond
Film Finances Ltd

Production Solicitors
Jonathan Berger, Mishcon De Reya

Insurance
Sampson & Allen

Arriflex Cameras/Zeiss Lenses Supplied by
Media Film Service London

Additional Camera Equipment
ICE

Lighting Equipment
Lee Lighting (Scotland) Ltd

Video Transfers
Midnight Transfer

Freight
Ecosse World Express

Stunt Arranger
Terry Forrestal

Stunt Performers
Tom Delmar, Nrinder Dhudwar, Richard Hammatt, Paul Heasman, Tom Lucy, Andreas Petrides

Animal Handler
David Stewart

Publicity
McDonald & Rutter

Thanks to
David Aukin, Allon Reich, Sara Geater, Carol Anne Docherty, Archie MacPherson, Jonathan Channon, Nicole Jacob, Kay Sheridan, Richard Findlay, @Tods Murray WS

Special Thanks to
David Bryce, Eamon Doherty and all at Calton Athletic Recovery Group for their inspiration and courage

Cast
Ewan McGregor
Mark Renton

Ewen Bremner
Daniel 'Spud' Murphy

Jonny Lee Miller
Simon, 'Sick Boy'

Kevin McKidd
Thomas 'Tommy' Mackenzie

Robert Carlyle
Francis Begbie

Kelly Macdonald
Diane

Peter Mullan
Swanney

James Cosmo
Mr Renton
Eileen Nicholas
Mrs Renton
Susan Vidler
Allison
Pauline Lynch
Lizzy
Shirley Henderson
Gail
Stuart McQuarrie
Gavin, US tourist
Irvine Welsh
Mikey Forrester
Dale Winton
game show host
Keith Allen
dealer
Kevin Allen
Andreas
Ann-Louise Ross
Gail's mother
Billy Riddoch
Gail's father
Fiona Bell
Diane's mother
Vincent Friell
Diane's father
Hugh Ross
Victor Eadie
men
Kate Donnelly
woman
Finlay Welsh
sheriff
Eddie Nestor
estate agent

Calton Athletic Football Club

[uncredited]
Andrew Macdonald
man looking for a flat let

8,142 feet
93 minutes

Dolby SRD
Colour by
Rank Film Laboratories

Credits compiled by Markku Salmi, BFI Filmographic Unit

Also Published

L'Argent
Kent Jones (1999)

Blade Runner
Scott Bukatman (1997)

Blue Velvet
Michael Atkinson (1997)

Caravaggio
Leo Bersani & Ulysse Dutoit
(1999)

Crash
Iain Sinclair (1999)

The Crying Game
Jane Giles (1997)

Dead Man
Jonathan Rosenbaum
(2000)

Don't Look Now
Mark Sanderson (1996)

Do the Right Thing
Ed Guerrero (2001)

Easy Rider
Lee Hill (1996)

The Exorcist
Mark Kermode (1997,
2nd edn 1998)

Independence Day
Michael Rogin (1998)

Last Tango in Paris
David Thompson (1998)

Once Upon a Time in America
Adrian Martin (1998)

Pulp Fiction
Dana Polan (2000)

The Right Stuff
Tom Charity (1997)

Saló or The 120 Days of Sodom
Gary Indiana (2000)

Seven
Richard Dyer (1999)

The Terminator
Sean French (1996)

Thelma & Louise
Marita Sturken (2000)

The Thing
Anne Billson (1997)

The 'Three Colours' Trilogy
Geoff Andrew (1998)

Titanic
David M. Lubin (1999)

The Wings of the Dove
Robin Wood (1999)

Women on the Verge of a Nervous Breakdown
Peter William Evans (1996)

WR – Mysteries of the Organism
Raymond Durgnat (1999)